ATTORNEY INTELLIGENCE

INK AND THINK: STRATEGIC INSIGHTS INTO CONTRACT MANAGEMENT AND NEGOTIATION

For Students, Legal Professionals, and Business Professionals

Version: 108

"Jai Shree Krishna"

"ॐ असतो मा सद्गमय। तमसो मा ज्योतिर्गमय। मृत्योर्मा अमृतं गमय॥"

"Aum Asato mā sadgamaya, tamaso mā jyotirgamaya, mṛityor mā amṛitaṃ gamaya!"

"Lead me from untruth to truth, from darkness (ignorance) to light (knowledge), from death to immortality!"

ACKNOWLEDGMENTS

My heartfelt gratitude to my parents, wife, kids and friends, thank you for your understanding during those late nights and free time spent writing. Your encouragement kept me motivated when doubts crept in, and your words of encouragement fuelled my determination to see this project through to completion.

I am truly blessed to have such amazing people in my life, and I dedicate this book to each and every one of you. Your presence in my life is a gift that I cherish deeply, and I am grateful for the love and support you have shown me.

With lots of love and appreciation...!!

Scope of the Book: "Contract Management Insights: Lessons from the Field"

This book explores the intricate world of contract management, offering a comprehensive look at its principles, practices, and real-world applications. Drawing from extensive experience and learnings, the book covers key areas of contract management.

The goal of this book is to serve as a practical guide for law students, contract managers, legal professionals, and business leaders. It provides actionable insights and tools to navigate the complexities of contract management effectively. By blending theoretical knowledge with practical experience, readers will gain a deep understanding of how to manage contracts successfully in today's dynamic business environment.

A contract management training program is designed to equip individuals with the knowledge and skills necessary to effectively manage contracts throughout their lifecycle. Such a program typically covers various aspects of contract management, including drafting, negotiation, administration, and compliance.

In today's dynamic business environment, effective contract management is crucial for maintaining robust legal and commercial relationships. This book from Attorney Intelligence provides a comprehensive understanding of contract management principles and practices. From drafting and negotiating agreements to ensuring compliance and mitigating risks, the insights guide readers through each stage of the contract lifecycle. Whether you are a legal professional or a business executive, mastering these skills will enhance your ability to manage contracts efficiently and achieve successful outcomes. Dive in and start transforming your contract management processes today.

TABLE OF CONTENTS

INTRODUCTION TO CONTRACTS MANAGEMENT:

Contract management is the process of overseeing and administering contracts between two or more parties to ensure that all parties fulfil their obligations and achieve the intended outcomes. It involves the efficient and effective management of contracts throughout their lifecycle, from initiation and negotiation to execution, performance monitoring, and closeout.

Example: Let's say you're running a marketing agency that frequently enters into contracts with clients for various services like social media management, advertising campaigns, and content creation. Efficient contract management is crucial to ensure smooth operations and maintain good relationships with clients.

Key aspects of contract management include:

1. **Contract Creation and Drafting:** Drafting clear, concise, and legally binding contracts that accurately reflect the parties' intentions and obligations.

2. **Negotiation:** Engaging in negotiations to reach mutually acceptable terms and conditions that satisfy the interests of all parties involved.

3. **Execution:** Ensuring that contracts are properly executed and legally binding, often involving the signing of agreements by authorized representatives.

4. **Performance Monitoring**: Tracking and monitoring the performance of contractual obligations to ensure compliance with terms and conditions, including deadlines, deliverables, and quality standards.

5. **Change Management:** Managing changes to contracts, including amendments, modifications, and variations, while ensuring that changes are documented, approved, and communicated effectively.

6. **Risk Management:** Identifying, assessing, and mitigating risks associated with contracts, including legal, financial, operational, and reputational risks.

7. **Compliance:** Ensuring compliance with legal and regulatory requirements, as well as internal policies and procedures, throughout the contract lifecycle.

8. **Relationship Management:** Building and maintaining positive relationships with stakeholders, including clients, suppliers, vendors, and internal departments, to foster trust and collaboration.

9. **Dispute Resolution:** Resolving disputes and conflicts that may arise during the contract lifecycle, using negotiation, mediation, arbitration, or other dispute resolution mechanisms.

10. **Closeout:** Properly closing out contracts upon completion or termination, including finalizing payments, documenting lessons learned, and ensuring that all obligations are fulfilled.

Effective contract management requires strong communication, negotiation, organizational, and analytical skills, as well as a thorough understanding of legal and regulatory requirements. It plays a critical role in optimizing business outcomes, mitigating risks, and fostering successful relationships between parties involved in contractual agreements.

Example:

Let's walk through a live example of a SaaS Agreement between a company, "iTechno Group LLP," and a customer, "AI Innovative Corp." We'll cover the entire contract lifecycle, from initiation to renewal/termination.

Step-by-Step Process

1. Initiation

- **Requirement Gathering:**

  a. iTechno Group LLP meets with AI Innovative Corp. to understand their need for a CRM SaaS solution.

b. They discuss AI Innovative Corp.'s business goals, specific features needed, and any compliance requirements.

- **Preliminary Discussions:**

a. They agree on a scope of work, initial pricing, service levels, and key deliverables.
b. An initial proposal is shared with AI Innovative Corp.

2. Contract Authoring

- **Template Selection:**

- iTechno Group LLP selects a standard SaaS agreement template that includes clauses on service levels, data privacy, uptime guarantees, and termination.

- **Customization:**

a. The contract is customized to include specific terms such as:

    i. Monthly subscription fee: $1,000
    ii. Service level agreement: 99.9% uptime
    iii. Support: 24/7 customer support
    iv. Data privacy: Compliance with GDPR and CCPA
    v. Term: 1 year with automatic renewal

3. Internal Review and Approval

- **Internal Stakeholder Review:**

a. The draft contract is reviewed by iTechno Group LLP's legal, finance, and operations teams.

b. Feedback is incorporated, and necessary revisions are made.

- **Approval Workflow:**

a. The contract is routed through iTechno Group LLP's automated approval workflow.

b. Final approval is obtained from senior management.

4. Negotiation

- **Customer Review:**

  a. The draft contract is sent to AI Innovative Corp. for review.

  b. AI Innovative Corp. requests some changes to the termination clause and additional data security measures.

- **Redlining and Revisions:**

  a. Using a contract management platform, both parties redline the contract to track changes.

  b. Terms are negotiated, and the contract is revised to include:

      i. **Termination clause:** Either party can terminate with 30 days' notice.

      ii. **Enhanced data security measures:** Regular security audits and encryption of data at rest and in transit.

- **Final Approval:**

  a. Both iTechno Group LLP and AI Innovative Corp. obtain final approval from their respective stakeholders.

5. Contract Execution

- **E-Signature Integration:**

  a. The final contract is sent for e-signature using DocuSign.

  b. Both parties sign the contract electronically.

- **Secure Storage:**

  a. The signed contract is stored in iTechno Group LLP's contract management system.

  b. Access controls and backup procedures are implemented.

6. **Obligation Management**

- **Service Delivery:**

    a. iTechno Group LLP begins delivering the CRM solution as per the contract terms.

    b. They monitor performance against the SLA using their internal monitoring tools.

- **Compliance Monitoring:**

    a. Regular checks are conducted to ensure compliance with GDPR and CCPA.

    b. Monthly reports are generated and shared with AI Innovative Corp.

7. **Performance Tracking and Reporting**

- **Performance Tracking:**

    a. Key metrics such as uptime, support response times, and user satisfaction are tracked.

    b. Any issues are addressed promptly to maintain service quality.

- **Analytics and Reporting:**

    a. Quarterly performance reports are generated and reviewed with AI Innovative Corp.

    b. Insights are used to optimize service delivery.

8. **Renewal/Termination**

- **Automated Renewals:**

    a. Three months before the contract term ends, AI Innovative Corp. receives an automated notification about the upcoming renewal.

    b. A renewal proposal is discussed and agreed upon.

- **Termination Management:**

    a. If AI Innovative Corp. decides not to renew, the contract termination process is initiated.

    b. iTechno Group LLP ensures all data is securely handed over and complies with termination procedures.

- **Archiving:**

    a. The expired contract is archived in the contract management system.

    b. Records are maintained for audit and compliance purposes.

Example Platforms:

1. **DocuSign CLM:** Used for contract creation, negotiation, execution, and storage.

2. **Salesforce:** CRM platform provided by iTechno Group LLP.

3. **Ironclad:** Contract lifecycle management tool for tracking and compliance.

This example illustrates how a SaaS contract is managed throughout its lifecycle, ensuring efficient, compliant, and transparent processes for both the company and the customer.

✱✱✱

<h1 style="text-align:center">SAMPLE: SOFTWARE AS A SERVICE (SaaS) AGREEMENT</h1>

This SaaS Agreement ("**Agreement**") is made effective as of April 1, 1993, by and between iTechno Group LLP, a California corporation with its principal place of business at 123 Tech Lane, San Francisco, CA 94105 ("**Provider**"), and AI Innovative Corp., a New York corporation with its principal place of business at 456 Innovation Drive, New York, NY 10001 ("**Customer**").

1. Definitions.

    a. "**Services**": The CRM software services provided by Provider to Customer as described in Exhibit A.

    b. "**SLA**": Service Level Agreement attached as Exhibit B.

    c. "**Effective Date**": The date on which this Agreement is signed by both parties.

    d. "**Term**": The duration of this Agreement, as defined in Section 7.

2. Services.

    a. Provider agrees to provide the Services to Customer as described in Exhibit A.

    b. Provider will ensure the Services comply with the SLA attached as Exhibit B.

3. Fees and Payment.

    a. Customer agrees to pay Provider a monthly subscription fee of $1,000.

    b. Payment is due on the first day of each month and shall be considered late if not received within 30 days of the due date.

4. Support and Maintenance.

    a. Provider will provide 24/7 customer support as described in Exhibit C.

b. Provider will maintain and update the software to ensure it remains compliant with applicable laws and performs as specified.

5. Data Privacy and Security.

a. Provider will comply with GDPR and CCPA requirements.

b. Provider will conduct regular security audits and encrypt data at rest and in transit.

6. Term and Termination.

a. This Agreement shall commence on the Effective Date and continue for a term of one (1) year, automatically renewing for additional one (1) year terms unless either party provides 30 days' written notice of non-renewal.

b. Either party may terminate this Agreement with 30 days' written notice.

c. Upon termination, Provider will securely return all Customer data and assist with the transition as described in Exhibit D.

7. Service Level Agreement (SLA).

a. Provider guarantees 99.9% uptime as detailed in the SLA attached as Exhibit B.

b. Penalties for failing to meet the SLA will be handled as described in Exhibit B.

8. Limitation of Liability

a. Provider's total liability under this Agreement shall not exceed the total amount paid by Customer in the twelve (12) months preceding the claim.

b. Provider shall not be liable for any indirect, incidental, special, or consequential damages.

9. Confidentiality.

   a. Both parties agree to maintain the confidentiality of each other's proprietary information.

   b. Confidential information shall not be disclosed to any third party without prior written consent.

10. Governing Law

This Agreement shall be governed by and construed in accordance with the laws of the State of New York, without regard to its conflict of laws principles.

11. Dispute Resolution

Any disputes arising out of or related to this Agreement shall be resolved through binding arbitration in New York, NY.

12. Miscellaneous

This Agreement constitutes the entire agreement between the parties and supersedes all prior agreements and understandings. Amendments or modifications to this Agreement must be in writing and signed by both parties.

IN WITNESS WHEREOF, the parties hereto have executed this SaaS Agreement as of the Effective Date.

iTechno Group LLP

By: _______________________

Name: ___________________

Title: ____________________

Date: ____________________

AI Innovative Corp.

By: _______________________

Name: ___________________

Title: ____________________

Date: ____________________

Exhibit A

Description of Services

- **CRM Software:** Access to Tech Solutions Inc.'s CRM platform with features including contact management, sales pipeline management, and reporting tools.

Exhibit B

Service Level Agreement (SLA)

- **Uptime Guarantee:** 99.9% uptime.
- **Penalty:** 5% credit of monthly fee for each 0.1% below the uptime guarantee.

Exhibit C

Support and Maintenance

- **Support:** 24/7 customer support via phone and email.
- **Maintenance:** Regular updates and bug fixes.

Exhibit D

Data Transition

- **Data Return:** Provider will return all Customer data within 30 days of termination.
- **Transition Assistance:** Provider will assist with data migration to a new platform as needed.

This template covers the key aspects of a SaaS contract and can be further customized based on the specific needs and agreements between iTechno Group Inc. and AI Innovative Corp.

****

LEGAL FOUNDATIONS IN CONTRACT MANAGEMENT:

Legal foundations in contract management are essential for ensuring that contracts are legally enforceable and effectively manage risks. These foundations encompass a range of principles and practices that help organizations draft, negotiate, execute, and monitor contracts in compliance with legal requirements and organizational policies.

Here's a breakdown of the key components under this category:

1. **Contract Law:** An understanding of the principles and rules of contract law that govern the formation, validity, interpretation, and enforcement of contracts. This includes:

   - **Offer and Acceptance:** The process by which one party makes an offer and the other party accepts it, thereby creating a legally binding agreement.

   - **Consideration:** The exchange of something of value (e.g., money, goods, services) between parties, which forms the basis of a contract.

   - **Capacity:** The legal ability of parties to enter into a contract, including factors such as age, mental capacity, and authority.

   - **Legality:** Contracts must involve lawful purposes and cannot violate public policy or engage in illegal activities.

Example: TechSolutions Inc. offers to develop custom software for RetailCorp for $100,000. RetailCorp accepts the offer. Both parties intend for this agreement to be legally binding, have the capacity to contract, and the purpose of the contract (software development) is legal.

2. **Common Contract Terms:** Familiarity with common contractual provisions and clauses used in various types of contracts. These may include:

   - **Payment terms:** Specifies the terms and conditions for payment, including amounts, methods, and timing.

- **Deliverables:** Describes the goods or services to be provided by each party under the contract.

- **Termination clauses:** Outlines the conditions under which the contract can be terminated, including notice periods and consequences.

- **Indemnification:** Allocates responsibility for losses, damages, or liabilities arising from the contract.

- **Confidentiality:** Protects sensitive information shared between parties during the contract term.

- **Governing law and jurisdiction:** Specifies the applicable law and jurisdiction for resolving disputes arising from the contract.

Example:

Confidentiality Clause: All confidential information disclosed by either party to the other shall be maintained in strict confidence and shall not be disclosed to any third party without prior written consent. This obligation shall remain in effect for three years post-termination of the contract.

3. **Key Legal Concepts:** Understanding key legal concepts relevant to contract management, including:

- **Breach of Contract:** Occurs when one party fails to fulfil its contractual obligations.

- **Damages:** Monetary compensation awarded to the injured party in case of a breach.

- **Indemnity:** One party agrees to compensate the other for certain losses or damages.

- **Warranties and Representations:** Statements of fact or promises made by one party to the other.

Example:

Breach of Contract: If TechSolutions Inc. fails to deliver the software on the agreed-upon date, RetailCorp can claim a breach of contract.

Damages: RetailCorp might seek damages for any losses incurred due to the delayed delivery.

Indemnity Clause: TechSolutions Inc. agrees to indemnify RetailCorp against any losses, damages, or liabilities arising from third-party claims of intellectual property infringement related to the software.

Warranties and Representations: TechSolutions Inc. warrants that the software will be free from defects for one year from the date of delivery and represents that it has the necessary rights and licenses to develop and deliver the software.

By understanding these legal foundations, contract managers can effectively draft, negotiate, interpret, and enforce contracts while minimizing legal risks and ensuring compliance with applicable laws and regulations.

****

CONTRACT LIFECYCLE MANAGEMENT (CLM):

Contract lifecycle management (CLM) involves overseeing contracts from their inception to their termination or renewal. Here's an overview of the stages involved in CLM:

1. **Initiation:** The contract lifecycle begins with the identification of a need or opportunity that requires a contractual arrangement. This stage involves defining the scope of work, identifying stakeholders, and assessing risks and requirements.

2. **Drafting:** Once the need for a contract is identified, parties begin drafting the contract terms and conditions. This stage involves defining the rights, obligations, and responsibilities of each party, as well as specifying key contractual provisions, such as pricing, deliverables, timelines, and dispute resolution mechanisms.

3. **Negotiation:** After drafting the initial contract, parties engage in negotiations to reach mutually acceptable terms. Negotiations may involve discussions on pricing, scope of work, terms and conditions, and other relevant aspects of the contract. Negotiation aims to address concerns, clarify ambiguities, and ensure that the contract reflects the interests of all parties involved.

4. **Execution:** Once negotiations are complete and all parties agree on the terms, the contract is executed. This involves obtaining signatures from authorized representatives of each party to formalize the agreement. Execution may also involve other formalities, such as notarization or witnessing, depending on legal requirements and the nature of the contract.

5. **Performance:** After execution, the parties begin performing their respective obligations under the contract. This stage involves monitoring and managing contract performance to ensure compliance with terms and conditions, including deadlines, quality standards, and deliverables. Contract managers track progress, address issues or deviations, and communicate with stakeholders as necessary to ensure successful implementation.

6. **Change Management:** Throughout the contract lifecycle, changes to the contract may be necessary due to evolving circumstances, unforeseen events, or changes in requirements. Change management involves identifying, evaluating, and managing changes to the contract through formal processes, such as change orders or amendments. It aims to ensure that changes are documented, approved, and implemented in accordance with the contract terms.

7. **Closeout:** At the end of the contract term or upon completion of the project, the contract enters the closeout stage. This involves finalizing any remaining activities, such as payments, deliverables, and documentation. Contract managers ensure that all obligations have been fulfilled, conduct post-contract reviews or evaluations, and formally close out the contract in accordance with agreed-upon procedures.

By effectively managing each stage of the contract lifecycle, organizations can optimize contract performance, minimize risks, and enhance overall contract outcomes.

INITIATION:
CONTRACT REQUESTS – BUSINESS REQUIREMENT OR BUSINESS NEED

Contract requests are formal submissions or proposals made to initiate the creation or modification of a contract. They typically occur at the beginning of the contract lifecycle and can come from various parties within an organization, such as departments, project managers, or procurement teams.

The requests can be classified into two categories:

1. **Corporate:** Generally, the requests under this category does not involve any costs or with minimum value involved. Agreements which fall under this category will be Non-Disclosure Agreement, Visitor NDA, Evaluation Agreements, Software Testing Agreements, etc.

2. **Commercial:** All the requests which involves commercial, cost and/or value under the Agreements falls under this category. Agreements such as Enterprise Software License Agreement, Statement of Works, Professional Services Agreements, Subscription Agreements, etc.

Here's an overview of the key components and considerations involved in contract requests:

Key Components of Contract Requests

1. **Requestor Information:**

   - **Details:** Name, department, and contact information of the person or team making the request.

   - **Purpose:** To identify and communicate with the primary point of contact.

2. **Purpose of the Contract:**

   - **Description:** A clear explanation of why the contract is needed.

- **Scope:** Outline the objectives, deliverables, and any specific requirements or constraints.

3. **Parties Involved:**

   - **Internal Parties:** Departments or individuals within the organization.

   - **External Parties:** Suppliers, contractors, clients, or other external entities.

4. **Key Terms and Conditions:**

   - **Duration:** Start and end dates of the contract.

   - **Payment Terms:** Pricing, payment schedule, and any related financial terms.

   - **Responsibilities:** Obligations and duties of each party.

   - **Deliverables:** Specific outputs or services to be provided.

5. **Attachments and Supporting Documents:**

   - **Proposals:** Preliminary proposals or quotations from the other party.

   - **Specifications:** Detailed specifications or requirements.

   - **Previous Contracts:** Copies of previous contracts if the new contract is a renewal or modification.

6. **Approval Workflow:**

   - **Signatories:** Names and roles of individuals who need to approve the request.

   - **Process:** Steps and sequence of approvals required before proceeding.

By following these practices and utilizing appropriate tools, organizations can streamline the contract request process, ensuring efficiency and reducing the risk of errors or omissions.

Examples:

1. Company A is into Software Development and want to sell their Software X to Company B. They want to provide the Software for evaluation to Company B.

2. Company Y (Pharma Sector) wants to partner with Company Z (Software Company) for developing software related to their vaccination program. Both companies working for first time, so they need a contract for new or future business.

✳✳✳

CONTRACT DRAFTING AND REVIEW:

Drafting clear, concise, and legally sound contracts is essential to ensure that the terms accurately reflect the intentions of the parties involved and mitigate potential disputes or misunderstandings. Similarly, effective contract review ensures that all parties understand their rights and obligations under the contract.

Once, you have all the information from client or business regarding the purpose, services and parties to the agreement. Understanding the business requirements is the key for Drafting any contract. Drafting can be done using either party template, in most of the cases the party who is on upper-hand or providing special services, will push for using their template.

Tip: We can always negotiate and push back to use our company templates, but always provide a strong rationale and convince the other party.

Here are some techniques for drafting and reviewing contracts:

Drafting Techniques:

1. **Use Templates and Precedents:** Utilize standardized contract templates and precedents to streamline the drafting process and ensure consistency across contracts. Tailor templates to specific requirements as necessary.

    a. **Categories:** Service agreement, purchase agreement, non-disclosure agreement (NDA), employment contract, etc.

    b. **Selection:** Indicate the type of contract to ensure the appropriate template and clauses are used.

2. **Define Clear Objectives:** Clearly define the objectives and scope of the contract to ensure that all parties have a common understanding of the purpose and goals.

3. **Use Plain Language:** Write in clear and simple language to avoid ambiguity and ensure that the contract is easily understandable by all parties.

4. **Be Specific and Detailed:** Clearly define the rights, obligations, and responsibilities of each party, including specifics such as deliverables, timelines, pricing, and performance standards.

5. **Avoid Ambiguity:** Use precise language and avoid vague or ambiguous terms that could lead to interpretation disputes. Define terms and concepts clearly to eliminate potential confusion.

6. **Include Essential Elements:** Ensure that the contract includes essential elements required for validity, such as offer, acceptance, consideration, and mutual assent.

7. **Anticipate Future Contingencies:** Consider potential future scenarios and include provisions for addressing changes, disputes, or unforeseen events through mechanisms such as dispute resolution clauses, termination clauses, and force majeure provisions.

8. **Comply with Legal Requirements:** Ensure that the contract complies with relevant laws, regulations, and industry standards. Consult legal experts as needed to verify legal compliance and mitigate legal risks.

9. **Balance Interests:** Strive to create a balanced agreement that meets the needs and interests of all parties involved, while also protecting your organization's interests.

10. **Review and Revise:** Review the draft contract carefully for accuracy, completeness, and consistency. Revise as needed to address any discrepancies or areas of concern.

Review Techniques:

1. **Thorough Examination:** Conduct a comprehensive review of the entire contract, paying attention to each provision and its implications.

2. **Legal Analysis:** Analyze the legal implications of each contract term, considering relevant laws, regulations, and judicial interpretations.

3. **Identify Risks:** Identify potential risks or liabilities associated with the contract terms and assess their impact on the organization.

4. **Verify Consistency:** Ensure that all contract terms are consistent with the agreed-upon terms and intentions of the parties, as well as with other related documents or agreements.

5. **Clarify Ambiguities:** Address any ambiguities or uncertainties in the contract language by seeking clarification from the parties involved or revising the wording as needed.

6. **Seek Input from Experts:** Consult legal experts or subject matter specialists to review complex or specialized contract terms and provide insights or recommendations.

7. **Consider Business Objectives:** Evaluate the contract terms in light of the organization's broader business objectives, ensuring alignment with strategic goals and priorities.

8. **Document Review Process:** Maintain records of the contract review process, including any revisions, comments, or recommendations made during the review.

By employing these techniques for drafting and reviewing contracts, organizations can create clear, comprehensive, and legally enforceable agreements that protect their interests and promote successful business relationships.

Examples:

1. Company A is into Software Development and want to sell their Software X to Company B. They want to provide the Software for trail or evaluation to Company B.
   – Draft Evaluation Agreement

2. Company Y (Pharma Sector) wants to partner with Company Z (Software Company) for developing software related to their vaccination program. Both companies working for first time, so they need a contract for new or future business.
   – Draft Non-Disclosure Agreement.

3. Company ABC Corporation is into OTT (Over-the-top) business providing television or film content over internet to all its subscribers.
   – Draft Subscription Agreement

4. Company Sri Krishna is into Education industry and want to purchase Stationary items throughout the year and want to procure all items from Company Lakshmi Books & Stationary.
    – Draft Master Agreement

5. Company Sri Krishna is into Education industry and want to purchase White Boards, Markers and Dusters every 3 months from Company Lakshmi Books & Stationary. **–
    Draft Statement of Work (SOW)**

CONTRACT NEGOTIATION/REDLINING SKILLS:

Developing effective negotiation skills is crucial for achieving favourable outcomes during contract negotiations. Here are some key strategies and tactics to enhance negotiation skills:

1. **Prepare Thoroughly:** Before entering negotiations, conduct comprehensive research and preparation. Understand your organization's goals, priorities, and constraints, as well as the interests and objectives of the other party. Anticipate potential issues or objections and develop strategies to address them.

2. **Establish Clear Objectives:** Define your negotiation objectives and priorities. Determine your ideal outcome as well as your acceptable alternatives and fallback positions. Establish clear targets for key terms and concessions.

3. **Build Rapport:** Foster a positive and collaborative atmosphere during negotiations by building rapport with the other party. Establishing trust and mutual respect can help facilitate constructive dialogue and problem-solving.

4. **Active Listening:** Listen actively to the other party's perspectives, concerns, and priorities. Seek to understand their underlying interests and motivations. Acknowledge their points and demonstrate empathy and understanding.

5. **Communicate Effectively:** Clearly communicate your own interests, needs, and priorities. Present your proposals in a concise and persuasive manner, highlighting the benefits and rationale behind your positions. Use persuasive language and compelling arguments to support your case.

6. **Focus on Interests, Not Positions:** Look beyond stated positions and focus on underlying interests and objectives. Explore potential areas of common ground and mutual benefit. Brainstorm creative solutions that meet the needs of both parties.

7. **Manage Emotions:** Keep emotions in check and maintain professionalism throughout the negotiation process. Stay calm, composed, and respectful, even in the face of disagreements or conflicts. Avoid personal attacks or confrontational behaviour.

8. **Negotiate Win-Win Solutions:** Strive to achieve mutually beneficial outcomes that satisfy the interests of both parties. Look for opportunities to create value and expand the pie rather than engaging in zero-sum competition.

9. **Use Concessions Wisely:** Make concessions strategically, based on a careful assessment of their value and importance. Prioritize your concessions and use them as bargaining chips to secure concessions from the other party in return.

10. **Stay Flexible and Adaptive:** Remain flexible and open to alternative solutions or compromises. Be prepared to adjust your strategy and tactics in response to new information, changing circumstances, or unexpected developments.

11. **Negotiate in Stages:** Break negotiations down into smaller, manageable stages and address one issue at a time. This can help prevent information overload and facilitate progress towards reaching agreement.

12. **Document Agreements:** Clearly document any agreements or commitments reached during negotiations. Summarize key terms and ensure that both parties have a clear understanding of their obligations.

CONTRACT REDLINING:

Contract redlining involves the process of reviewing, editing, and negotiating the terms of a contract. The term "**redlining**" comes from the practice of marking up the document, traditionally in red ink, to highlight changes and comments. Modern software tools now facilitate this process digitally.

Key Concepts in Contract Redlining

1. **Track Changes:**

   - **Purpose:** To document all edits made to the contract.

   - **Tools:** Most word processors (like Microsoft Word) and contract management software have a "Track Changes" feature that allows multiple parties to see who made which changes and when.

2. **Comments and Annotations:**

- **Purpose:** To explain the rationale behind changes or to ask questions about specific parts of the contract.
- **Usage:** Comments are often used to suggest alternative wording, seek clarification, or flag issues for further discussion.

3. **Version Control:**

- **Purpose:** To manage different versions of the contract during the negotiation process.

- **Best Practices:** Keep a clear record of each version to avoid confusion. Ensure all parties are working from the most recent version.

4. **Key Clauses to Review:**

- **Scope of Work:** Ensure the responsibilities and deliverables are clearly defined.

- **Payment Terms:** Confirm the terms of payment, including amounts, schedules, and conditions.

- **Confidentiality:** Review clauses related to the protection of sensitive information.

- **Termination:** Understand the conditions under which the contract can be terminated by either party.

- **Dispute Resolution:** Check the methods outlined for resolving any disputes that may arise.

5. **Negotiation Tactics:**

- **Collaborative Approach:** Aim for a win-win situation where both parties feel satisfied with the agreement.

- **Prioritize Issues:** Focus on the most critical terms first. Be willing to compromise on less critical issues.

- **Clear Communication:** Maintain open lines of communication to address concerns promptly and clearly.

Tools for Contract Redlining:

1. **Microsoft Word:** Widely used with robust track changes and commenting features.

2. **Google Docs:** Allows real-time collaboration and editing.

3. **Specialized Software:** Tools like ContractWorks offer advanced features for contract management, including redlining, e-signatures, and more.

Best Practices:

1. **Maintain Professionalism**: Keep the language formal and respectful, even when negotiating contentious points.

2. **Detail-Oriented Review:** Pay close attention to detail to avoid overlooking critical terms or clauses.

3. **Legal Counsel:** Involve legal professionals to ensure the contract is legally sound and to get expert advice on complex issues.

4. **Consistent Updates:** Regularly update all stakeholders on the status of the contract and any major changes.

By honing these negotiation/redlining skills and adopting effective strategies and tactics, contract managers can enhance their ability to negotiate favourable outcomes and build positive, mutually beneficial relationships with counterparties.

Contract Negotiation & Redlining Case Study:

Analyzing real-world contract management scenarios through case studies and interactive exercises is an effective way to reinforce learning and apply theoretical knowledge to practical situations. Here are a few examples of case studies and exercises:

- **Scenario:** A client is negotiating a contract with a vendor for the supply of raw materials. The negotiation involves pricing, delivery schedules, quality standards, and payment terms.

Here's a detailed context for redlining during vendor contract negotiation:

Key Areas to Redline and Context:

1. **Scope of Work (SOW)**

Original Clause: "Vendor shall provide IT support services to the client as per the terms agreed."

Redlined Clause: "Vendor shall provide comprehensive IT support services to the client ~~terms agreed,~~ **including but not limited to network maintenance, software updates, and helpdesk support, as per the detailed terms agreed upon in Exhibit A."**

> Add a comment with justification for redlining (so that the other party will understand your logic of addition or deletion).
>
> For example: We would like explicitly mention the support services provided by you that are covered under Exhibit A.

Context: Clarify the specific services included to avoid any ambiguity and ensure that both parties have a mutual understanding of the scope.

2. **Payment Terms**

Original Clause: "Client shall pay the vendor within 30 days of receiving the invoice."

Redlined Clause: "Client shall pay the vendor within ~~30~~45 days of receiving ~~thea~~ **correct and undisputed** invoice. **Invoices shall be submitted monthly, and any discrepancies must be resolved within 15 days of receipt.**"

> Add a comment with justification for redlining (so that the other party will understand your logic of addition or deletion).
>
> For example: Our company policy is that we will be making the payment to all our vendors within 45 days from the invoice receipt date.

Context: Adjust payment terms to better align with the client's payment cycle and add provisions for handling disputed invoices.

3. Confidentiality

Original Clause: "The vendor agrees to keep all client information confidential."

Redlined Clause:" The vendor agrees to keep all client information confidential _and shall not disclose any confidential information to third parties without the prior written consent of the client, except as required by law. This obligation shall survive the termination of this agreement for a period of five years._"

> Comment: We need additional protection in case of accidental disclosures to any third-party with our consent.

Context: Specify the duration of the confidentiality obligation and conditions under which information may be disclosed.

4. Termination Clause

Original Clause: "Either party may terminate the contract with 30 days' notice."

Redlined Clause: "Either party may terminate the contract with 60 days' written notice. _In the event of a breach of any material term, the non-breaching party may terminate this agreement immediately upon written notice if the breach is not cured within 30 days of notification._"

> Comment: We want be notified in writing of any termination and in case of breach we need to immediately terminate the contract.

Context: Extend the notice period for termination and include provisions for termination in the event of a material breach.

5. Limitation of Liability

Original Clause: "The vendor's liability shall be limited to the amount paid by the client under this contract."

Redlined Clause:" The vendor's liability shall be limited to the amount paid by the client under this contract<u>, except in cases of gross negligence, wilful misconduct, or breach of confidentiality, where liability shall not be limited.</u>"

> Comment: We want unlimited liability in case of breach or gross negligence.

Context: Carve out exceptions where the limitation of liability would not apply, such as in cases of gross negligence or wilful misconduct.

6. Intellectual Property (IP):

Original Clause: "All intellectual property developed during the term of this contract shall belong to the client."

Redlined Clause: "All intellectual property developed <u>specifically for the client</u> during the term of this contract shall belong to the client. <u>Any pre-existing IP or tools used by the vendor in the course of providing services shall remain the property of the vendor</u>."

> Comment: All the IP rights under this Agreement will be owned by parties, who developed or provided any such information.

Context: Clarify ownership of IP, distinguishing between what is developed specifically for the client and what is pre-existing or independently developed by the vendor.

7. Indemnification:

Original Clause: "The vendor shall indemnify the client against any third-party claims."

Redlined Clause: "Either party ~~The vendor~~ shall indemnify <u>and hold harmless</u> the ~~client~~<u> other party and its officers, directors, employees, and agents</u> against any third-party claims <u>arising out of the vendor's gross negligence, wilful misconduct, or breach of this agreement. The client shall indemnify the vendor against any third-party claims arising out of the client's gross negligence or wilful misconduct.</u>"

> Comment: Making this section mutual and add additional terms for clarity.

Context: Define the scope of indemnification more clearly and include mutual indemnification provisions.

General Tips for Redlining:

Clarity and Precision: Ensure that all changes are clear and unambiguous to avoid future disputes.

Consistency: Maintain consistency in terminology and definitions throughout the contract.

Review Legal Implications: Consult with legal counsel to understand the implications of changes and to ensure compliance with relevant laws.

Negotiation Mindset: Approach redlining as a negotiation tool, aiming for a balanced agreement that protects the interests of both parties.

Document Version Control: Keep track of different versions of the contract to ensure that all changes are documented and agreed upon by both parties.

2.   Case Study: Contract Dispute Resolution

- **Scenario**: A construction project is delayed due to disputes between the contractor and subcontractors over scope changes, delays, and payment issues.

To address the disputes between the contractor and subcontractors in your construction project, it is essential to review and revise the contract clauses that govern scope changes, delays, and payment issues. Here is a structured approach to redlining the contract for dispute resolution:

1. Scope Changes

Context: Disputes over scope changes often arise from unclear communication and lack of agreement on adjustments in cost and time. The revised clause ensures clear communication, advance notice, and a mutual agreement on changes.

Original Clause: "The Contractor may, at any time, by written order, make changes in the work within the general scope of the Contract. If such changes cause an increase or decrease in the cost or time required for performance of the work, an equitable adjustment shall be made in the Contract price or delivery schedule, or both."

Redlined Clause: "The Contractor may, at any time, by written order, make changes in the work shall ~~notify may, at any time, by written order, make changes in the work~~ shall notify the Subcontractor in writing of any proposed changes in the work within the general scope of the Contract. <u>Such notification must be provided at least 10 business days in advance of the intended change date.</u> If such changes cause an increase or decrease in the cost or time required for performance of the work, <u>the Subcontractor must submit a detailed proposal for the</u> ~~an~~ equitable adjustment <u>shall be made</u> in the Contract price or delivery schedule~~, or both~~ <u>within 5 business days of receiving the change notification. The equitable adjustment shall be mutually agreed upon in writing before any work on the change is commenced.</u>"

> Add a comment with justification for redlining (so that the other party will understand your logic of addition or deletion).
>
> For example: We want written notification of any such change in advance and the change should be approved by both parties.

2. **Delays:**

Context: Delays in construction projects can lead to significant conflicts. The revised clause aims to establish a clear process for notification and negotiation of new deadlines, allowing for adjustments due to unforeseen circumstances.

Original Clause: "If the Subcontractor fails to complete the work within the time specified in the Contract, the Contractor may, without prejudice to other rights or remedies, terminate the Contract or any part thereof."

Redlined Clause: "If the Subcontractor fails to complete the work within the time specified in the Contract<u>, the Subcontractor must notify the Contractor immediately in writing, providing reasons for the delay and a proposed new completion date. The Contractor and Subcontractor shall meet within 3 business days to discuss the delay and agree on a revised completion schedule. If the delay is caused by factors beyond the Subcontractor's control, the completion time shall be equitably adjusted</u>. ~~t~~<u>T</u>he Contractor may, without prejudice to other rights or remedies, terminate the Contractor any part thereof <u>if no agreement can be reached within 10 business days.</u>"

> Add a comment:
> For example: If there is any delay in work completion by subcontractor, they should provide a written notification with the reasons and remedy.

3. Payment Issues:

Context: Payment issues are common sources of conflict in construction projects. The revised clause specifies a timeline for payments and dispute notification to ensure transparency and fairness.

Original Clause: "Payments shall be made to the Subcontractor upon submission of invoices and approval by the Contractor."

Redlined Clause: "Payments shall be made to the Subcontractor <u>within 30 days</u> upon submission of invoices and approval by the Contractor. <u>The Contractor shall provide written notification of any invoice disputes within 10 business days of receipt. If an invoice is disputed, the Contractor shall pay the undisputed portion of the invoice within the 30-day period. Any disputes over payment shall be resolved through the Dispute Resolution clause outlined below.</u>"

> Add a comment: Here, the redlines are self-explanatory, so if you want you can skip the comment and further provide your rationale if the other party insists.

4. Dispute Resolution

Context: A structured dispute resolution process helps avoid lengthy and costly legal battles. The revised clause introduces a stepwise approach to resolve conflicts amicably before resorting to arbitration.

Original Clause: "Any disputes arising under this Contract shall be resolved by arbitration."

Redlined Clause: "Any disputes arising under this Contract shall be resolved by ~~arbitration~~ <u>through the following process:</u>

a. Negotiation: The Contractor and Subcontractor shall first attempt to resolve the dispute through direct negotiation. Either party may initiate the negotiation by providing written notice to the other party, outlining the nature of the dispute and a proposed resolution.

b. Mediation: If the dispute is not resolved within 10 business days of the written notice, the parties agree to submit the dispute to mediation before a mutually agreed-upon mediator. The mediation shall be held within 20 business days of the initial mediation request.

c. Arbitration: If the dispute is not resolved through mediation, the parties agree to submit the dispute to binding arbitration under the rules of the American Arbitration Association. The arbitration decision shall be final and binding on both parties, and judgment upon the award may be entered in any court having jurisdiction."

Summary: The revised clauses are designed to provide clarity, promote fair dealings, and facilitate timely resolution of disputes, thereby minimizing disruptions to the construction project. These changes emphasize the importance of communication, mutual agreement, and structured processes for handling scope changes, delays, and payment issues. Legal counsel should review these revisions to ensure they align with relevant laws and contractual norms.

***

CONTRACT RISK MANAGEMENT:

Risk management is a critical aspect of contract management, involving the identification, assessment, and mitigation of risks associated with contracts. Here's how to effectively manage risks throughout the contract lifecycle:

1. **Identify Risks:** Begin by identifying potential risks associated with the contract. This includes considering various factors such as legal, financial, operational, and reputational risks. Review the contract terms, scope of work, and potential challenges that may arise during performance.

2. **Assess Risks:** Evaluate the likelihood and potential impact of each identified risk. Use qualitative and quantitative methods to assess risks, considering factors such as probability, severity, and vulnerability. Prioritize risks based on their significance and potential consequences.

3. **Legal Risks:** Assess legal risks associated with the contract, including non-compliance with laws and regulations, contractual disputes, intellectual property issues, and liability exposure. Consult legal experts to identify potential legal pitfalls and ensure that contract terms are legally enforceable and compliant.

4. **Financial Risks:** Evaluate financial risks related to the contract, such as cost overruns, payment disputes, currency fluctuations, and financial instability of counterparties. Conduct financial analysis and due diligence to assess the financial health and stability of parties involved in the contract.

5. **Operational Risks:** Consider operational risks that may impact the successful implementation of the contract, such as resource constraints, technology failures, supply chain disruptions, and changes in market conditions. Develop contingency plans and risk mitigation strategies to address operational challenges.

6. **Reputational Risks:** Assess reputational risks that could arise from the contract, including negative publicity, damage to brand reputation, and stakeholder dissatisfaction. Monitor stakeholder perceptions and proactively address issues that may affect the organization's reputation.

7. **Mitigate Risks:** Once risks are identified and assessed, develop risk mitigation strategies to reduce the likelihood and impact of potential threats. This may involve implementing preventive measures, transferring risks through insurance or contractual arrangements, or accepting risks within tolerance levels.

8. **Contractual Protections:** Include contractual provisions that address specific risks and allocate responsibilities between parties. This may include indemnification clauses, limitation of liability provisions, warranties, and insurance requirements.

9. **Monitoring and Control:** Continuously monitor risks throughout the contract lifecycle and implement controls to mitigate emerging risks. Establish clear communication channels and escalation procedures to address issues promptly.

10. **Contingency Planning:** Develop contingency plans and alternative courses of action to manage risks if they materialize. Anticipate potential scenarios and have predefined strategies in place to respond effectively.

11. **Review and Update:** Regularly review and update risk management plans in response to changing circumstances, new information, or lessons learned from previous contracts. Incorporate feedback and insights to improve risk management practices over time.

By systematically identifying, assessing, and mitigating risks associated with contracts, organizations can minimize potential disruptions, protect their interests, and enhance the likelihood of successful contract outcomes.

Case Study: Contract Risk Assessment

- This case is presented with a series of contract clauses and scenarios related to liability, indemnification, termination, and force majeure.

Here's a detailed context for redlining during vendor contract negotiation:

a. Liability:

Scenario: A subcontractor damages equipment on a construction site, and there is ambiguity in the contract regarding liability for such damages.

Original Clause: "The Contractor shall not be liable for any damages arising out of or in connection with this contract."

Redlined Clause: "The Contractor shall not be liable for <u>any indirect, incidental, or consequential</u> damages arising out of or in connection with this contract. <u>However, the Contractor shall be liable for direct damages caused by its gross negligence or wilful misconduct.</u>"

Rationale: Clarifies that the Contractor is not liable for indirect damages. Specifies liability for direct damages caused by gross negligence or wilful misconduct.

b. Indemnification:

Scenario: The subcontractor faces a lawsuit from a third party due to an incident on the construction site. The subcontractor seeks indemnification from the contractor.

Original Clause: "The Subcontractor agrees to indemnify and hold harmless the Contractor from any claims, damages, or liabilities arising out of the Subcontractor's work."

Redlined Clause: "The Subcontractor agrees to indemnify and hold harmless the Contractor from any claims, damages, or liabilities arising out of the Subcontractor's work<u>, except to the extent such claims, damages, or liabilities result from the Contractor's gross negligence or wilful misconduct. The Contractor shall indemnify and hold harmless the Subcontractor for claims, damages, or liabilities arising from the Contractor's gross negligence or wilful misconduct</u>."

Rationale: Limits the Subcontractor's indemnification obligation to exclude damages resulting from the Contractor's gross negligence or wilful misconduct. Adds a reciprocal indemnification obligation for the Contractor.

c. Termination:

Scenario: The contractor wants to terminate the contract due to the subcontractor's repeated delays and poor performance.

Original Clause: "The Contractor may terminate this contract at any time for convenience with a 30-day notice."

Redlined Clause: "The Contractor may terminate this contract at any time for convenience with a 30-day notice. _In the event of termination for cause due to the Subcontractor's repeated delays, poor performance, or breach of contract, the Contractor shall provide written notice specifying the cause and allow the Subcontractor 10 business days to cure the breach. If the Subcontractor fails to cure the breach within this period, the Contractor may terminate the contract immediately._"

Rationale: Adds a cure period for the Subcontractor to remedy breaches before termination for cause. Specifies immediate termination if the Subcontractor fails to cure the breach.

d. Force Majeure:

Scenario: A natural disaster delays the construction project, and there is a need to clarify the responsibilities of both parties during such events.

Original Clause: "Neither party shall be liable for any failure to perform due to force majeure events."

Redlined Clause: "Neither party shall be liable for any failure to perform due to force majeure events_, including but not limited to acts of God, war, terrorism, labour strikes, or natural disasters. The affected party must notify the other party in writing within 5 business days of the occurrence of the force majeure event. Both parties shall use reasonable efforts to mitigate the effects of the force majeure event and resume performance as soon as practicable. If the force majeure event continues for more than 30 days, either party may terminate the contract with written notice._"

Rationale: Defines force majeure events and the notification requirement. Includes a mitigation obligation and a termination option if the event continues for an extended period.

These revisions aim to balance the responsibilities and protections for both parties, ensuring clarity and fairness in the contract terms. Legal counsel should review these changes to ensure they are enforceable and compliant with relevant laws and regulations.

CONTRACT ADMINISTRATION:

Administering contracts effectively is crucial for ensuring that all parties fulfil their obligations and that the project progresses smoothly. Here are some best practices for contract administration:

1. **Clear Documentation:** Maintain detailed records of the contract, including the original agreement, amendments, correspondence, and any changes made during the project.

2. **Obligation Tracking:** Create a system to track all obligations outlined in the contract. This could include deliverables, milestones, payment schedules, and any other commitments.

3. **Regular Communication:** Maintain open communication channels with all parties involved in the contract. Regular updates and meetings can help address issues promptly and ensure that everyone is on the same page.

4. **Performance Monitoring:** Establish metrics for evaluating performance and regularly assess whether the contractor is meeting the agreed-upon standards. This could involve site visits, progress reports, or other methods of monitoring.

5. **Change Management:** Implement a formal process for managing changes to the contract. Any modifications should be documented, agreed upon by all parties, and communicated clearly to avoid misunderstandings.

6. **Dispute Resolution Mechanism:** Include a mechanism for resolving disputes in the contract, such as mediation or arbitration. Having a predetermined process can help prevent conflicts from escalating and minimize disruptions to the project.

7. **Risk Management:** Identify potential risks associated with the contract and develop strategies for mitigating them. This could involve insurance coverage, contingency plans, or other risk management techniques.

8. **Compliance Monitoring:** Ensure that all parties adhere to relevant laws, regulations, and industry standards throughout the duration of the contract.

9. **Performance Incentives:** Consider incorporating performance incentives into the contract to encourage the contractor to meet or exceed expectations. This could include bonuses for early completion or penalties for delays.

10. **Documentation of Changes:** Document any changes to the contract in writing and ensure that all parties sign off on them. This helps prevent misunderstandings and provides a clear record of the agreement.

By implementing these best practices, you can effectively administer contracts, minimize risks, and ensure the successful completion of projects.

Case Study: Contract Performance Monitoring

- **Scenario:** Company XYZ, a leading technology firm, entered into a service agreement with ABC Solutions, a provider of IT support services. The contract detailed various performance metrics, including response times, resolution times, and customer satisfaction scores, which were crucial for maintaining high service standards.

1. **Response Time:**

    Original Language: Response to critical issues within 4 hours.

    Redlined Language: Response to critical issues within 42 hours.
    (Reduced time to enhance service level and customer satisfaction.)

    Reason: To ensure critical issues are addressed more promptly, minimizing potential disruptions and enhancing customer confidence in the service.

2. **Resolution Time:**

    Original Language: Issues to be resolved within 36 hours.

    Redlined Language: Issues to be resolved within 3624 hours.
    (Shortened resolution time to ensure quicker problem resolution and minimize downtime.)

Reason: To accelerate issue resolution, reducing downtime and improving overall service efficiency. This change was based on feedback indicating that prolonged issues were causing significant operational disruptions.

3. Customer Satisfaction:

Original Language: Minimum satisfaction score of 80%.

Redlined Language: Minimum satisfaction score of ~~80~~90%.
(Increased target to push for higher service quality and better customer experience.)

Reason: To set a higher benchmark for service quality. This was driven by a strategic goal to differentiate ABC Solutions as a premium service provider through exceptional customer satisfaction.

Implementation

1. Monitoring Tools:

An advanced contract management software was implemented to automate the tracking of these revised metrics. This software provided real-time data and alerts for any deviations from the agreed standards.

2. Regular Reviews:

Weekly performance review meetings were established to discuss the metrics. These meetings included representatives from both companies, ensuring transparency and collaboration.

3. Feedback Mechanism:

A feedback loop was created where end-users could directly report their satisfaction levels and any issues faced. This data was fed into the performance monitoring system for real-time analysis.

Results:

- **Improved Response and Resolution Times:**

The average response time decreased from 4 hours to 1.5 hours, and the resolution time improved from 36 hours to 20 hours, surpassing the contract requirements.

- **Increased Customer Satisfaction:**
Customer satisfaction scores rose from 80% to 92%, indicating a significant improvement in service quality.

- **Enhanced Transparency and Trust:**

Regular reviews and transparent communication fostered a stronger partnership between Company XYZ and ABC Solutions. Issues were addressed promptly, and continuous improvements were made based on the feedback received.

Conclusion

The implementation of a structured contract performance monitoring system, along with the revised metrics, allowed Company XYZ to ensure ABC Solutions met their service obligations effectively. This case study highlights the importance of clear metrics, automated monitoring tools, and regular communication in managing contract performance. By adopting these practices, organizations can achieve better compliance, higher service quality, and improved stakeholder satisfaction.

All the above case studies and exercises engage participants in practical, hands-on learning experiences that simulate real-world contract management challenges. By analyzing scenarios, applying theoretical concepts, and collaborating with peers, participants develop critical thinking, communication, and problem-solving skills essential for effective contract management

COMPLIANCE AND ETHICS:

Compliance with legal and regulatory requirements is essential in contract management to ensure that all parties involved operate within the bounds of the law and adhere to industry standards. Additionally, ethical considerations play a crucial role in maintaining integrity and trust in business relationships. Here's why compliance and ethics are important in contract management:

1. **Legal Obligations:** Contracts are legally binding agreements, and failure to comply with their terms can result in legal consequences such as breach of contract claims, financial penalties, or litigation. Compliance with relevant laws and regulations helps mitigate these risks and ensures that contracts are enforceable.

2. **Risk Management:** Compliance with legal and regulatory requirements reduces the risk of potential disputes, lawsuits, or regulatory actions that could arise from non-compliance. By understanding and adhering to legal obligations, organizations can protect their reputation and financial interests.

3. **Ethical Considerations:** Contract management involves not only following the letter of the law but also upholding ethical standards and principles. Ethical behaviour fosters trust and goodwill among parties and promotes long-term, sustainable business relationships.

4. **Transparency and Accountability:** Ethical contract management practices promote transparency and accountability in business dealings. Parties should provide accurate and honest information, disclose conflicts of interest, and act in the best interests of all stakeholders.

5. **Corporate Social Responsibility (CSR):** Compliance with ethical standards extends beyond legal requirements to encompass broader societal expectations. Organizations are increasingly expected to consider the social and environmental impacts of their actions and ensure that their contracts align with CSR principles.

6. **Maintaining Trust and Reputation:** Ethical conduct in contract management is essential for building and maintaining trust with customers, suppliers, employees, and

other stakeholders. A reputation for integrity can enhance a company's brand value and competitiveness in the marketplace.

7. **Employee Morale and Engagement:** Ethical behaviour within an organization fosters a positive work environment, improves employee morale, and enhances employee engagement. Employees are more likely to be committed and motivated when they perceive that their organization operates with integrity and ethical principles.

8. **Avoiding Unforeseen Consequences:** Non-compliance with legal and ethical standards can lead to unforeseen consequences, including damage to relationships, loss of business opportunities, and financial harm. By prioritizing compliance and ethics, organizations can mitigate these risks and promote sustainable growth.

In summary, compliance with legal and regulatory requirements and adherence to ethical considerations are critical aspects of contract management. By integrating these principles into contract management processes, organizations can minimize risks, foster trust, and uphold their reputation and values.

Case Study: Compliance Audit

- **Scenario**: An organization conducts a compliance audit of its contracts to ensure adherence to legal and regulatory requirements, including data privacy, anti-corruption, and intellectual property rights.

Let's consider a specific scenario where an organization conducts a compliance audit of its contracts to ensure adherence to data privacy, anti-corruption, and intellectual property rights requirements. Here are three clauses from the original contract and their redlined versions after the compliance audit.

Contract: Agreement between ABC Corp and XYZ Ltd

1. **Data Privacy:**

   Original Language:

   - XYZ Ltd will collect and store customer data as necessary for service delivery.

- XYZ Ltd agrees to use reasonable measures to protect customer data.

Redlined Language:

- XYZ Ltd will collect, ~~process,~~ and store customer data as necessary for service delivery, **in full compliance with applicable data protection laws, including but not limited to the GDPR and CCPA**.

- XYZ Ltd agrees to ~~use~~ **implement and maintain** reasonable measures, **appropriate technical and organizational measures** to protect customer data **against unauthorized access, use, disclosure, alteration, or destruction**.

- **XYZ Ltd will notify ABC Corp within 24 hours of any data breach that involves customer data.**

Reason for Redlines:

- **Compliance with Specific Laws:** The clause is updated to specifically mention GDPR and CCPA to ensure compliance with major data protection laws.

- **Enhanced Security Measures:** The term "reasonable measures" is replaced with "appropriate technical and organizational measures" to specify a higher standard of data protection.

- **Breach Notification:** A requirement for breach notification within 24 hours is added to ensure prompt response to data breaches.

2. **Anti-Corruption:**

Original Language:
- Both parties agree to comply with applicable laws.

Redlined Language:

- **Both parties agree to comply with all applicable laws, including but not limited to the Foreign Corrupt Practices Act (FCPA) and the UK Bribery Act.**

- <u>XYZ Ltd represents and warrants that it has not made, and will not make, any payments or gifts of value to any government official, political party, or candidate for political office for the purpose of obtaining or retaining business.</u>

- <u>XYZ Ltd will maintain accurate books and records in accordance with generally accepted accounting principles, and will provide ABC Corp with reasonable access to such records upon request.</u>

Reason for Redlines:

- **Specific Laws:** Explicitly mentioning FCPA and UK Bribery Act ensures compliance with key anti-corruption regulations.

- **Prohibition of Bribery:** A clause is added to explicitly prohibit bribery and corruption.

- **Record-Keeping and Access:** Requirements for accurate record-keeping and providing access to these records are included to enhance transparency and accountability.

3. **Intellectual Property:**

Original Language:

- Any intellectual property developed during the term of this agreement will be jointly owned by ABC Corp and XYZ Ltd.

Redlined Language:

- <u>Any intellectual property developed during the term of this agreement will be jointly owned by ABC Corp and XYZ Ltd owned solely by ABC Corp. XYZ Ltd agrees to assign and hereby assigns all rights, title, and interest in such intellectual property to ABC Corp.</u>

- **XYZ Ltd will refrain from using ABC Corp's intellectual property, including trademarks, copyrights, and patents, without prior written consent from ABC Corp.**

- **XYZ Ltd will indemnify, defend, and hold harmless ABC Corp from and against any claims, damages, liabilities, costs, and expenses (including reasonable attorneys' fees) arising from any alleged infringement of intellectual property rights related to the services provided under this agreement.**

- **Both parties will maintain the confidentiality of all proprietary information disclosed during the term of this agreement and thereafter.**

Reason for Redlining:

- **Ownership Clarification:** The ownership clause is changed to ensure ABC Corp retains sole ownership of any developed intellectual property.

- **Use Restriction:** Added a clause to prevent XYZ Ltd from using ABC Corp's IP without permission.

- **Indemnification:** An indemnity clause is added to protect ABC Corp against IP infringement claims.

- **Confidentiality:** Added a clause to ensure the confidentiality of proprietary information.

By redlining the contract in this manner, the organization ensures that it addresses key compliance areas related to data privacy, anti-corruption, and intellectual property rights, thereby reducing legal and regulatory risks.

****

TECHNOLOGY TOOLS:

Contract management software and technology tools have become essential for streamlining contract processes, improving efficiency, and reducing risks associated with manual management. Here's an introduction to some key technology tools used in contract management:

1. **Contract Lifecycle Management (CLM) Software:** CLM software automates and centralizes the entire contract lifecycle, from creation and negotiation to execution, storage, and analysis. It typically includes features such as contract drafting templates, electronic signatures, version control, alerts and notifications, and reporting capabilities.

2. **Electronic Signature Platforms:** Electronic signature platforms allow parties to sign contracts digitally, eliminating the need for printing, scanning, and mailing physical documents. These platforms offer secure and legally binding signature solutions, expediting the signing process and reducing administrative burdens.

3. **Document Management Systems (DMS):** DMS platforms provide a centralized repository for storing, organizing, and managing contract documents. They offer version control, access controls, search functionalities, and audit trails to ensure that contracts are securely stored and easily retrievable when needed.

4. **Contract Authoring Tools:** Contract authoring tools assist in creating standardized contract templates and clauses, streamlining the drafting process, and ensuring compliance with legal and regulatory requirements. They often feature libraries of pre-approved clauses, customizable templates, and contract assembly wizards.

5. **Contract Analytics and AI:** Contract analytics and artificial intelligence (AI) tools leverage natural language processing (NLP) and machine learning algorithms to extract insights from contract data, identify risks and opportunities, and improve decision-making. These tools can analyze contract language, identify trends, and flag potential compliance issues or inconsistencies.

6. **Vendor Management Systems (VMS):** VMS platforms help organizations manage relationships with suppliers and vendors by facilitating contract creation, performance tracking, compliance monitoring, and invoice management. They centralize vendor data and streamline communication and collaboration between parties.

7. **Compliance Management Software:** Compliance management software assists organizations in tracking and ensuring compliance with legal and regulatory requirements across their contracts. It provides tools for managing regulatory updates, assessing compliance risks, and monitoring adherence to contract terms.

8. **Integration with ERP and CRM Systems:** Contract management software often integrates with enterprise resource planning (ERP) and customer relationship management (CRM) systems to streamline processes and enhance data visibility. Integration allows for seamless exchange of information between contract management and other business systems.

9. **Mobile Apps:** Many contract management software solutions offer mobile apps that enable users to access contracts, review documents, track tasks, and collaborate with stakeholders on the go. Mobile accessibility enhances flexibility and productivity for users working remotely or in the field.

10. **Blockchain Technology:** Blockchain-based contract management solutions offer enhanced security, transparency, and immutability by recording contract transactions on a decentralized ledger. Blockchain can help prevent fraud, tampering, and disputes by providing a verifiable record of contract actions and changes.

These technology tools empower organizations to optimize their contract management processes, improve compliance, mitigate risks, and drive operational efficiency in today's increasingly complex business environment.

Examples of Contract Management Software and Technology Tools:

- **DocuSign:** Facilitates electronic signatures and secure document exchange.

- **ContractWorks:** Offers document storage, tracking, and reporting features.

- **iCertis:** Provides contract lifecycle management with AI-driven insights.

- **Concord:** Enables collaboration, e-signatures, and contract tracking.

- **Agiloft:** Offers customizable contract management workflows and automation.

- **PandaDoc:** Streamlines document creation, collaboration, and signing processes.

- **SAP Ariba:** Integrates procurement and contract management functions.

- **Conga:** Combines document generation, contract management, and e-signatures.

- **SpringCM:** Manages contract workflows, compliance, and document storage.

- **CobbleStone:** Provides comprehensive contract lifecycle management and analytics.

These tools help organizations streamline contract processes, ensure compliance, and enhance overall efficiency.

Continuous Learning and Professional Development

Continuous learning and professional development are essential for contract managers to stay abreast of industry trends, regulatory changes, and best practices.

Here are some strategies to encourage ongoing learning and development in contract management:

1. **Training Programs:** Attorney Intelligence offers regular training sessions, workshops, or seminars on topics such as contract law, negotiation techniques, risk management, and contract administration.

2. **Certification Programs:** Encourage contract managers to pursue professional certifications such as Certified Commercial Contracts Manager (CCCM) or Certified Federal Contracts Manager (CFCM) offered by organizations like the National Contract Management Association (NCMA). Certification programs provide comprehensive training and validation of skills and knowledge in contract management.

3. **Online Courses and Webinars:** Provide access to online courses, webinars, and e-learning platforms that cover a wide range of contract management topics. Platforms like Attorney Intelligence, Coursera, Udemy, or LinkedIn Learning offer courses on contract law, contract drafting, procurement practices, and compliance management.

4. **Industry Conferences and Events:** Support attendance at industry conferences, seminars, and networking events where contract managers can learn from industry experts, participate in panel discussions, and exchange best practices with peers. These events provide valuable opportunities for professional development and networking.

5. **Professional Associations Memberships:** Encourage contract managers to join professional associations such as the National Contract Management Association (NCMA), International Association for Contract and Commercial Management (IACCM), or Association of Corporate Counsel (ACC). Membership provides access to resources, publications, webinars, and networking opportunities within the contract management community.

6. **Mentorship Programs:** Establish mentorship programs where experienced contract managers can provide guidance, advice, and career development support to junior staff. Mentorship helps foster knowledge transfer, skill development, and professional growth within the organization.

7. **Cross-Functional Collaboration:** Encourage contract managers to collaborate with colleagues from other departments such as legal, finance, procurement, and operations. Cross-functional collaboration provides exposure to different perspectives, promotes knowledge sharing, and enhances understanding of how contracts impact various aspects of the business.

8. **Industry Publications and Journals:** Encourage contract managers to subscribe to industry publications, journals, and newsletters that provide updates on legal developments, regulatory changes, case studies, and best practices in contract management. Examples include Contract Management Magazine, The Journal of Contract Management, and Harvard Business Review.

9. **Internal Knowledge Sharing:** Facilitate internal knowledge sharing sessions where contract managers can present case studies, share lessons learned, and discuss challenges and solutions with colleagues. Peer-to-peer learning enhances collaboration, builds a culture of continuous improvement, and fosters innovation within the organization.

By accessing to resources, networking opportunities, and industry updates, contract managers can foster a culture of continuous learning and professional development that empowers contract managers to excel in their roles and drive business success.

***

ADDITIONAL TIPS:

A. How to Redline a Document in Microsoft Word:

1. Open the Document:

- o Open the document you want to edit in Microsoft Word.

2. Enable Track Changes:

- o Go to the **Review** tab on the Ribbon.

- o Click on **Track Changes**. This will enable the tracking of all changes you make to the document. You can also use the shortcut "**Ctrl + Shift + E**".

3. Customize Track Changes Options:

- o In the "**Review**" tab, click on the small arrow next to "**Track Changes**" to open a drop-down menu.

- o Select "**Track Changes Options**" to customize how changes are displayed. You can choose different colours for insertions, deletions, and formatting changes.

4. Make Edits:

- o Start editing the document. All changes will be highlighted in different colours or underlined/strikethrough based on your Track Changes settings.

- o Insertions will typically be shown with underlined text, while deletions will be shown with strikethrough text.

5. Add Comments:

- o To add a comment, highlight the text you want to comment on.

- o Click on "**New Comment**" in the "**Review**" tab, or right-click the highlighted text and select "**New Comment**."

- o Type your comment in the comment box that appears in the margin.

6. **Review Changes:**

   o To review the changes, go to the Review tab.
   o Use the "**Next**" and "**Previous**" buttons in the Changes group to navigate through each change.

   o Use "**Accept**" or "**Reject**" to approve or disapprove each change.

7. **Display for Review:**

   You can choose how to display the changes using the "**Display for Review**" drop-down menu:

   o **Simple Markup:** Displays a clean view of the document with indicators where changes have been made.

   o **All Markup:** Shows all changes inline and in the margins.

   o **No Markup:** Displays the document as if all changes were accepted.

   o **Original:** Displays the original document without any changes.

8. **Compare Documents (if needed):**

   o If you have two versions of a document and want to see the changes between them, you can use the Compare feature:

   a. Go to the Review tab.

   b. Click on Compare in the Compare group.

   c. Choose Compare to compare two versions of a document.

   d. Select the original and revised documents to see a detailed comparison.

9. **Save the Document:**

   o Save your document regularly to ensure that all changes are recorded.

- o When you're done, you can save a final version by accepting all changes and turning off Track Changes.

Example: Original and Redlined Versions

Original Contract Excerpt

1. Response Time:

Response to critical issues within 4 hours.

2. Resolution Time:

Issues to be resolved within 36 hours.

3. Customer Satisfaction:

Minimum satisfaction score of 80%.

Redlined Contract Excerpt

1. Response Time:

~~Response to critical issues within 4 hours.~~
Critical issues response time should be within 2 hours.

2. Resolution Time:

~~Issues to be resolved within 36 hours.~~
Resolution time for any issues should be resolved within 24 hours.

3. Customer Satisfaction:

~~Minimum satisfaction score of 80%.~~
The minimum score needs to be 95% for any customer satisfaction.

Finalizing the Document

1. Accept/Reject All Changes:

Once all reviews are complete, you can accept or reject all changes at once by clicking on the arrow under the "**Accept**" or "**Reject**" button and selecting "**Accept All Changes**" or "**Reject All Changes**."

2. Delete All Comments:

To delete all comments, click on the arrow under "**Delete**" in the "**Comments**" group and select "**Delete All Comments in Document**."

By following these steps, you can effectively manage redlining in Microsoft Word, ensuring that all changes and comments are accurately tracked and reviewed.

✷✷✷

B. Contract GAP Analysis:

Comparing two (1:1) contracts: A contract gap analysis involves a systematic review and comparison of an existing contract against a desired or required standard, such as legal requirements, industry standards, or best practices. Here's how you can approach it:

- **Identify the Existing Contract:** Start by obtaining a copy of the current contract that you want to analyze. Ensure it is the latest version and includes all relevant amendments and attachments.

- **Understand Requirements:** Clearly define what standards or requirements you are comparing the contract against. This could include legal requirements, company policies, industry standards, or specific contractual obligations.

- **Review the Existing Contract:** Carefully examine each section and clause of the contract. Note down provisions related to scope, terms, obligations, rights, responsibilities, warranties, liabilities, termination clauses, and any other relevant areas.

- **Identify Gaps:** Compare each provision in the existing contract against the desired or required standards. Note any inconsistencies, deficiencies, ambiguities, or areas where the contract does not meet the standard.

- **Document Findings:** Document your findings in a structured manner. Clearly outline each identified gap, specifying the section of the contract where the gap exists and detailing how it fails to meet the standard or requirement.

- **Assess Impact:** Evaluate the potential impact of each identified gap. Consider legal risks, compliance issues, operational impacts, financial implications, and other relevant factors.

- **Recommendations:** Based on your analysis, propose recommendations for addressing each identified gap. This could involve drafting amendments, renegotiating terms, seeking legal advice, or other corrective actions.

- **Implementation Plan:** Develop an implementation plan to address the identified gaps. Assign responsibilities, set timelines, and outline the steps needed to revise the contract or take other necessary actions.

- **Monitor and Review:** After making changes or implementing corrective actions, monitor the contract to ensure that gaps have been adequately addressed. Regularly review the contract to ensure ongoing compliance with standards and requirements.

- **Documentation:** Maintain comprehensive documentation throughout the process, including your analysis, findings, recommendations, implementation plan, and any correspondence related to the contract.

By following these steps, you can conduct a thorough contract gap analysis to ensure that your contracts align with legal requirements, industry standards, and organizational expectations.

This process is important because it ensures that the contract meets all legal and business requirements, reduces risks, and avoids potential disputes. Thorough analysis ensures that all necessary clauses are included, making the contract fair and beneficial for all parties involved.

Contract GAP Analysis is required in several scenarios, including:

Negotiating the Agreement Template: The decision of whether to use your own template or a third-party template.

Mergers and Acquisitions: Ensuring all contracts align with the new business structure and regulatory requirements.

Regulatory Compliance: Verifying contracts meet updated legal and regulatory standards.

Renewals and Renegotiations: Identifying areas for improvement or adjustment in contract terms.

Risk Management: Spotting potential risks and ensuring appropriate safeguards are in place.

Project Management: Ensuring contracts align with project goals and deliverables.
Vendor and Supplier Agreements: Ensuring terms are favourable and compliant with organizational policies.

Internal Audits: Regularly reviewing contracts to maintain standards and avoid discrepancies.

Conducting a Contract GAP Analysis helps maintain the integrity and effectiveness of contractual agreements across various business operations.

Example of Contract GAP Analysis:

Scenario: TechSolutions Inc. and RetailCorp Contract for Software Development

Background:

TechSolutions Inc. and RetailCorp have an existing contract for the development of a custom software solution for inventory management. During a compliance review, RetailCorp's legal team identified potential gaps in the contract that could expose the company to risks.

Steps in Contract GAP Analysis:

1. Identify Contract Requirements
2. Review Existing Contract
3. Identify Gaps
4. Assess Impact and Prioritize Gaps
5. Develop Action Plan to Address Gaps

1. Identify Contract Requirements

- **Objective:**

To ensure that the contract covers all necessary aspects to protect both parties and meet regulatory requirements.

- **Key Areas to Cover:**

- Scope of Work
- Payment Terms
- Confidentiality
- Data Privacy
- Intellectual Property
- Dispute Resolution
- Termination Clauses
- Compliance with Laws

2. Review Existing Contract

- **Method:**

Conduct a thorough review of the existing contract to determine if it addresses all identified requirements.

3. Identify Gaps

Gap Analysis Findings:

- **Data Privacy:**

Existing Clause: "All personal data collected under this Agreement shall comply with applicable data protection laws."

Gap: The clause is vague and does not specify particular data protection measures or laws.

- **Intellectual Property:**

Existing Clause: "All intellectual property rights in the software developed shall be owned by TechSolutions Inc."

Gap: The clause does not address the rights of RetailCorp to use, modify, or transfer the software.

- **Dispute Resolution:**

Existing Clause: Not explicitly addressed.

Gap: Lack of a clear dispute resolution mechanism.

- **Termination Clauses:**

Existing Clause: "Either party may terminate the contract with 30 days' notice."

Gap: No specifics on termination for breach, force majeure, or termination costs.

4. **Assess Impact and Prioritize Gaps**

    Impact Assessment:

    Data Privacy Gap: High impact due to potential non-compliance with regulations (e.g., GDPR), leading to fines and legal action.

    Intellectual Property Gap: Medium impact as it could limit RetailCorp's ability to fully utilize the software.

    Dispute Resolution Gap: High impact as it could lead to prolonged and unresolved disputes.

    Termination Clauses Gap: Medium impact due to potential ambiguities in contract termination scenarios.

5. **Develop Action Plan to Address Gaps**

    Action Plan:

    Data Privacy:
    Amended Clause: "All personal data collected, used, or processed under this Agreement shall comply with applicable data protection laws, including but not limited to the GDPR. Each party shall implement appropriate technical and organizational measures, such as encryption and access controls, to protect personal data. Each party shall promptly notify the other of any data breaches involving personal data processed under this Agreement."

    Intellectual Property:
    Amended Clause: "All intellectual property rights in the software developed under this Agreement shall be owned by TechSolutions Inc. RetailCorp shall have a non-exclusive, non-transferable, royalty-free license to use, modify, and transfer the software for its internal business purposes. TechSolutions Inc. warrants that the software does not infringe any third-party intellectual property rights and agrees to indemnify RetailCorp against any claims of infringement."

Dispute Resolution:
New Clause: "Any disputes arising out of or in connection with this Agreement shall be resolved through mediation in accordance with the rules of the American Arbitration Association. If the dispute cannot be resolved through mediation, it shall be submitted to binding arbitration."

Termination Clauses:
Amended Clause: "Either party may terminate the contract with 30 days' notice. In addition, either party may terminate the contract immediately for cause, including material breach or insolvency. In the event of termination for cause, the breaching party shall be liable for any termination costs incurred by the non-breaching party. Force majeure events shall allow either party to terminate the contract if such events prevent performance for more than 60 days."

Summary:
Conducting a Contract GAP Analysis involves a systematic review of an existing contract to identify any missing or inadequate provisions that could expose the parties to risks. By addressing these gaps with specific and detailed clauses, organizations can enhance the contract's robustness, ensure compliance with legal requirements, and better protect their interests. In this example, the analysis identified gaps in data privacy, intellectual property, dispute resolution, and termination clauses, leading to the development of a comprehensive action plan to address these issues.

Negotiating the Agreement Template:

In contract negotiations, the decision of whether to use your own template or a third-party template involves several considerations:

Control and Familiarity: Using your own template gives you control over the terms and conditions that align with your business practices and preferences. It also ensures familiarity among your team members.

Efficiency: A well-established internal template can streamline the negotiation process as it likely reflects your organization's standard terms, potentially reducing back-and-forth discussions.

Legal Compliance: Ensure that your own template meets current legal standards and regulatory requirements relevant to your industry and jurisdiction.

Adaptability: Consider using a third-party template if it offers provisions that better suit specific requirements or if it's commonly accepted in your industry, potentially facilitating smoother negotiations with external parties.

Risk Management: Evaluate the risks associated with both options, such as potential gaps in your own template or the need for extensive revisions of a third-party template to meet your needs.

Scenario:
You are negotiating a service agreement with a new vendor for IT support services.

Using Your Own Template:

Advantages:

Control: Your own template reflects your company's standard terms and conditions, which you and your legal team are familiar with.

Efficiency: Negotiations may proceed faster as both parties are likely familiar with your standard terms, reducing the need for extensive revisions.

Compliance: Your template can be tailored to meet specific regulatory requirements or industry standards relevant to IT services.
Example: You decide to use your company's standard service agreement template. It includes clauses on data protection, service levels, and termination procedures that have been vetted by your legal team to comply with relevant data privacy laws and industry best practices. This familiarity helps streamline negotiations and ensures that your company's interests are well-protected.

Using a Third-Party Template:

Advantages:

Industry Acceptance: A reputable third-party template may be widely recognized and accepted in your industry, potentially facilitating quicker agreement as it's already familiar to the vendor.

Best Practices: Third-party templates often incorporate industry best practices and standards that could enhance the contract's comprehensiveness.

Neutral Ground: Using a neutral template may signal openness to compromise and cooperation, fostering a positive negotiating atmosphere.

Example: You consider using a widely used IT service agreement template from a reputable industry association. This template includes provisions on liability limits, intellectual property rights, and dispute resolution mechanisms that are commonly accepted in the IT services sector. Using this template may expedite negotiations with the vendor who is also familiar with and comfortable with these terms.

Choosing Between Them:

Decision Factors: Your decision hinges on factors such as the complexity of the agreement, the need for customization, your company's risk tolerance, and the familiarity of the other party with your preferred template.

Hybrid Approach: In some cases, you may opt for a hybrid approach by starting with your own template and integrating beneficial provisions from a third-party template to address specific needs or industry standards.

In conclusion, whether to use your own template or a third-party template in contract negotiations depends on balancing control, efficiency, industry standards, and the specific requirements of the transaction or relationship.

C. Contracts Abstraction & Summarization:

Contracts are vital for businesses as they outline and govern the rights and responsibilities in any new relationship or agreement. As businesses grow, managing these contracts becomes more complex due to the increasing number and details involved.

Contract Abstraction simplifies this complexity by distilling key information, such as dates or important clauses, into a clear summary. This process highlights the most crucial terms, making it easier to grasp the essential details of the agreement. This summary is called a contract abstract.

The contract abstraction process is essential for effectively managing business relationships governed by contracts, whether with partners, suppliers, customers, or employees. To achieve long-term financial success, organizations must invest in a robust contract management process that includes contract abstraction. The specific stages of this process may vary depending on the organization's size and existing procedures. Here are the common steps typically involved in contract abstraction:

1. **Format Creation:**

    Establishing a structured format for contract abstraction, often using a question-and-answer approach to standardize the process.

2. **Contract Review:**

    Conducting a thorough review of each contract document to identify critical areas and key information.

3. **Contract Analysis:**

    Evaluating and interpreting contract clauses to understand their implications fully. This stage is crucial for developing a comprehensive understanding of the contract's nuances and potential legal risks.

4. **Information Abstraction:**

    Abstracting essential information identified during the review and analysis stages into a clear, readable format or template. This summary, known as the contract abstract, highlights key terms, obligations, rights, and other significant details. It should include references to specific page numbers or sections for easy reference.

By following these steps, organizations streamline their contract management processes, enhance clarity and accessibility of contract details, and mitigate legal risks associated with contract interpretation and compliance. This structured approach ensures that all stakeholders can easily access and understand the critical aspects of their contractual obligations and rights.

Why Is Contract Abstraction Important?

Contracts can be lengthy (sometimes hundreds of pages), making effective contract management a daunting task. By abstracting dates, clauses, payment terms and other key information, legal teams can save time and resources while ensuring compliance and increasing the team's overall productivity.

By implementing contract abstraction processes into your contract management framework, contracts become easier to read for non-legal professionals, as the essential clauses and key information is summarised and brought to the forefront. The contract management process becomes more convenient and simpler, while also making each contract accessible to the wider business.

When Is Contract Abstraction Used?

Contract abstraction is utilized across industries and businesses worldwide due to the sheer volume of contracts involved in everyday operations. In modern business relationships, contracts are standard and essential. However, managing contracts doesn't conclude once they are signed; crucial information necessary for informed decision-making remains within these documents.

Contracts often contain extensive legal jargon and lengthy sentences, which can obscure critical details and complicate their interpretation, especially for those outside the legal team. This complexity underscores the importance of contract abstraction in the contract management lifecycle.

Contract abstraction serves a vital role in both law firms and businesses by simplifying lengthy and intricate documents into concise summaries of key points. This transformation makes contracts more accessible and understandable to all stakeholders within the organization. It enhances clarity, streamlines legal processes, and facilitates compliance, ultimately supporting better business practices and decision-making.

What Industries are Contract Abstraction Services Popular With?

Contract abstraction services are widely favoured across various industries today. With contracts governing approximately 80% of B2B transactions, they have become integral to everyday business operations. However, contracts often pose challenges due to their complexity and extensive legal terminology, making interpretation difficult for many businesses.

Businesses across industries increasingly rely on contract abstraction services to enhance their understanding of contractual agreements. By simplifying contracts and extracting key information such as obligations, rights, and key dates, contract abstraction facilitates clearer comprehension and accessibility.

Industries ranging from healthcare and finance to technology and manufacturing benefit significantly from contract abstraction. These services not only save time but also empower organizations to make informed decisions based on comprehensive contract insights. By streamlining the interpretation process, contract abstraction supports improved operational efficiency and compliance across diverse business sectors.

Contract Abstraction Vs. Contract Summarisation

Contract abstraction and contract summarization both aim to distil the essential aspects of a contract, but they serve different purposes and are suited to different types of contracts:

Contract Summarization:

Contract summarization involves condensing the important points of a contract into a concise summary. It captures the key information from the entire contract, making it easier to grasp quickly and act as a reference. This approach is ideal for shorter contracts where the goal is to restate the main points succinctly for better understanding.

Contract Abstraction:

On the other hand, contract abstraction focuses on longer, more complex contracts. It involves extracting critical details such as rights, obligations, and liabilities into a brief summary. Rather than summarizing the entire contract, abstraction highlights the key points that are crucial for decision-making and compliance. This process is more comprehensive and detailed, providing deeper insights into contractual obligations and risks.

In essence, contract summarization simplifies shorter contracts for quick reference, while contract abstraction delves into the complexities of longer contracts to extract and clarify essential information. Each method serves to enhance understanding and facilitate effective contract management based on the specific needs and complexities of the contracts involved.

Contract Abstraction Vs. Contracts Vetting:

Contract abstraction simplifies contracts by extracting important information into a clear summary that's easy to understand. It focuses on highlighting key terms and essential details to provide a snapshot of the contract's contents.

In contrast, contract vetting involves a detailed examination of documents before they are signed and executed. This process ensures that all legal requirements are met, roles and responsibilities are defined clearly, and there are adequate legal protections and remedies in place. Contract vetting results in a due diligence of the document's clauses against potential risks and ensure compliance with legal standards.

Example of Contracts Abstraction & Summarization:

Scenario:

XYZ Corporation has signed a complex supply agreement with ABC Inc. for the delivery of raw materials over the next two years. The original contract is 50 pages long and includes detailed terms on pricing, delivery schedules, quality standards, penalties, and termination conditions.

a. **Contract Abstraction:**

Original Clause:

1.2 Pricing: The price for the raw materials will be $500 per metric ton, subject to adjustments based on market fluctuations. Payments will be made within 30 days of invoice receipt. Late payments will incur a penalty of 1.5% per month.

Sheet 1: Contract Abstraction

Section	Clause	Abstracted Information
1.2	Pricing	$500/metric ton, adjustable per market. Payment due: 30 days post-invoice. Late payment penalty: 1.5%/month.

b. Contract Summarization:

Sheet 2: Summary of Key Points:

Parties Involved:	XYZ Corporation (buyer), ABC Inc. (supplier).
Contract Duration	2 years.
Pricing:	$500 per metric ton, subject to market adjustments.
Payment Terms:	30 days from invoice receipt.
Late Payment Penalty:	1.5% per month.
Delivery Schedule:	Monthly deliveries, with adjustments for holidays.
Quality Standards:	Materials must meet ISO 9001 standards.
Termination Conditions:	Either party can terminate with 60 days' notice for breach of contract.

Benefits:

- **Abstraction:** Provides a quick reference to specific, essential details within the contract, such as pricing and payment terms.

- **Summarization:** Offers a broad overview of the entire contract, making it easier for stakeholders to understand key points without reading all 50 pages.

Application:

- **For Legal Teams:** Abstraction helps lawyers quickly find and review critical terms.

- **For Non-Legal Teams:** Summarization enables business managers to grasp the essential elements of the agreement without needing a detailed legal background.

By employing contract abstraction and summarization, XYZ Corporation can manage their agreement with ABC Inc. more effectively, ensuring that all critical terms are easily accessible and understandable for all relevant parties.

****

D. Contract Version Control:

Contract version control means keeping track of different versions of a contract as it goes through changes and updates. It ensures that every modification or revision made to the contract is recorded and managed properly. This helps maintain clarity and consistency in the contract, which is important when multiple people are reviewing and approving changes. By keeping a clear record of all versions, organizations can follow how the contract has changed over time, handle negotiations better, and reduce risks of confusion or disagreements over contract terms.

Example: Imagine a company, ABC Inc., negotiating a contract with a supplier for the supply of raw materials. Initially, they draft a contract specifying terms like price, delivery schedules, and quality standards. This draft is labelled as Version 1.

ABCInc_XYZCorp_MSA_2024-04-01_**V1.0**

During negotiations, ABC Inc. and the supplier agree to revise the delivery schedule to accommodate seasonal demand fluctuations. This change is documented in Version 2 of the contract, clearly indicating the modification and the reasons behind it.

ABCInc_XYZCorp_MSA_2024-04-01_**V2.0**

Later, ABC Inc. identifies an error in the pricing section of Version 2 that needs correction. They make the necessary adjustments and document these changes in Version 3 of the contract.

ABCInc_XYZCorp_MSA_2024-04-01_**V3.0**

Throughout this process, contract version control ensures that each iteration (Version 1, Version 2, Version 3, etc.) is tracked, dated, and stored appropriately. This allows ABC Inc. to maintain a clear record of changes made during negotiations, ensuring transparency and accountability. It also provides a history of the contract's evolution, aiding in audits, compliance checks, and dispute resolution if necessary.

Note: The format for version control varies between companies; some examples include Version 1.0, Version 0.1, Ver 2.0, Ver 0.2, V3.0, V0.3, v4.0, v0.4, and so on.

E. Contract Naming Convention:

Contract naming conventions refer to the standardized rules or guidelines used to name and label contracts systematically. These conventions help organizations organize and manage their contracts efficiently, ensuring clarity and ease of access. And this differs from organization to organization.

Here's an example of contract naming convention:

[Contract Type]_[Counterparty Name]_[Date]_[Version].

[Company Name]_[Counterparty Name]_[Contract Type]_[Date]_[Version].

[Date]_[Company Name]_[Counterparty Name]_[Contract Type]_[Version].

For instance, a contract between ABC Inc. and XYZ Corporation signed on July 1, 2024, could be named:

Services_ABC Inc_XYZ Corporation_2024-07-01_V1.

In this example:

Services: Indicates the type of contract (e.g., Services, Sales, Purchase).
ABC Inc: Name of the contracting party.
XYZ Corporation: Name of the counterparty.
2024-07-01: Date of contract execution.
V1: Version number of the contract.

Following such a convention ensures that contracts are easily identifiable, organized chronologically, and can be quickly retrieved when needed. This helps in maintaining order, tracking revisions, and facilitating efficient contract management within organizations.

***

F. NON-DISCLOSURE AGREEMENT:

A Non-Disclosure Agreement (NDA) is a simple contract between two or more parties that agrees to keep certain information confidential. It's like a promise to keep a secret. It is also referred to as Confidentiality Agreement or Proprietary Agreement.

Example:
Think of situation, where **Person A** have a unique recipe for sweet dish and it is shared with **Person B**, who wants to start a Confectionary Shop. **Person A** makes **Person B** sign an NDA to ensure **Person B** don't share **Person A** recipe with anyone else or use it in any way other than to make the sweet dish for his Shop. If **Person B** tells the recipe to someone else or uses it for something other than the making the sweet dish for his Shop, then **Person B** would be breaking the NDA and he would be liable of damages.

In today's business world, NDAs (Non-Disclosure Agreements) are essential for establishing and maintaining relationships between two or more parties. Before any business can proceed, an NDA is often signed to protect shared confidential information. There are different types of NDAs, including Unilateral NDA, Mutual NDA, and Visitor NDA, each tailored to specific business needs.

- **Unilateral NDA:** This type favours one party, setting terms that benefit one side. For instance, a software development company selling its software to a customer may use a Unilateral NDA to place all obligations and liabilities on itself, not the customer.

- **Mutual NDA:** This type applies to both parties, ensuring both share rights and obligations. For example, when a company and a vendor sign a Mutual NDA, both can exchange confidential information to understand each other's business better.

- **Visitor NDA:** This type is used when visitors, such as customers, auditors, or stakeholders, come to your office. They sign this NDA to protect your physical or digital infrastructure from unauthorized disclosure.

SAMPLE: Mutual NDA

This mutual Non-Disclosure Agreement (the "**Agreement**") is entered into as of August 15, 2024 (the "**Effective Date**"), by and between Attorney Intelligence LLP, with a principal place of business at Suite # 108, Santa Clara, CA 8001 (the "**Company**"), and Moral Science Ltd., with a principal place of business at #501, New York, NY 20021 (the "**Customer**"). The Disclosing Party and the Receiving Party may each be referred to as a "**Party**" or collectively as the "**Parties**."

1. Definition of Confidential Information.

1.1 For purposes of this Agreement "**Confidential Information**" means any information that is disclosed by either Party (the "**Disclosing Party**") to the other Party (the "**Receiving Party**"), in any form (whether written, oral, electronic, or other) and that is designated as confidential, proprietary, or with a similar designation, or that by its nature should reasonably be understood to be confidential. Confidential Information includes, but is not limited to:

a. Business plans, strategies, forecasts, and analyses.

b. Financial information, including pricing and cost data.

c. Technical data, product plans, designs, specifications, software, and research and development.

d. Customer and supplier information, including customer lists, contact information, and customer requirements.

e. Marketing and sales information, including strategies, marketing materials, and advertising plans.

f. Personnel information, including employee data, compensation, and organizational structure.

g. Any other information that is either marked or otherwise identified as confidential or proprietary, or that the Receiving Party should reasonably understand to be confidential.

1.2 Confidential Information does not include information that:

a. Is or becomes publicly known through no breach of this Agreement by the Receiving Party;

b. Is already known to the Receiving Party at the time of disclosure as evidenced by the Receiving Party's written records;

c. Is rightfully obtained by the Receiving Party from a third party without breach of any confidentiality obligation;

d. Is independently developed by the Receiving Party without use of or reference to the Disclosing Party's Confidential Information, as evidenced by written records; or

e. Is disclosed with the prior written approval of the Disclosing Party.

2. **Obligations of Receiving Party.**

2.1. The Receiving Party agrees to:

a. Maintain the Confidential Information in strict confidence and use the same degree of care as it employs to protect its own confidential information of like nature, but in no event less than a reasonable degree of care.

b. Use the Confidential Information solely for the purpose of evaluating a potential or existing business relationship with the Disclosing Party (the "**Purpose**").

c. Restrict disclosure of Confidential Information to its employees, agents, contractors, and other representatives who have a need to know such information for the Purpose and who are bound by written obligations of confidentiality and non-use at least as protective as those set forth herein.

d. Not disclose Confidential Information to any third party without the prior written consent of the Disclosing Party.

2.2. The Receiving Party shall immediately notify the Disclosing Party of any unauthorized use or disclosure of Confidential Information and take all reasonable steps to prevent further unauthorized use or disclosure.

3. **Return or Destruction of Confidential Information.**

Upon termination of this Agreement or upon the Disclosing Party's written request, the Receiving Party shall promptly return or destroy all documents and other tangible materials representing the Confidential Information and all copies thereof. The Receiving Party shall provide a written certification of such return or destruction upon request by the Disclosing Party.

4. No Grant of Rights.

Nothing in this Agreement shall be construed as granting any rights, by license or otherwise, to the Receiving Party under any intellectual property rights of the Disclosing Party, nor shall this Agreement grant the Receiving Party any rights in or to the Confidential Information except as expressly set forth herein.

5. Term and Termination.

5.1. This Agreement shall commence on the Effective Date and shall continue in effect until terminated by either party upon thirty (30) days' written notice to the other party.

5.2. The Receiving Party's duty to protect the Confidential Information shall survive the termination of this Agreement and shall remain in effect for a period of five (5) years following the date of termination and information related to source code or related technical information shall remain in effect in perpetuity.

6. Legal and Equitable Remedies.

The Receiving Party acknowledges that any breach of this Agreement may cause irreparable harm to the Disclosing Party, for which damages may not be an adequate remedy, and therefore the Disclosing Party shall be entitled to seek injunctive relief with respect thereto in addition to any other remedies.

7. Warranty.

7.1. Each Party warrants that it has the right to make the disclosures under this Agreement.

7.2. The Disclosing Party warrants that it believes in good faith that the Confidential Information disclosed under this Agreement is accurate and reliable. However, the Disclosing Party makes no representation or warranty, express or implied, as to the accuracy or completeness of the Confidential Information.

7.3. The Disclosing Party shall not be liable for any damages arising from the use of the Confidential Information by the Receiving Party.

8. Governing Law and Jurisdiction.

This Agreement shall be governed by and construed in accordance with the laws of the State of California, without regard to its conflict of laws principles. Any disputes arising out of or in connection with this Agreement shall be resolved exclusively in the courts located in Santa Clara County, California.

9. Miscellaneous.

9.1. **Entire Agreement:** This Agreement constitutes the entire agreement between the parties regarding the subject matter hereof and supersedes all prior or contemporaneous agreements, understandings, and communications, whether written or oral.

9.2. **Amendments:** This Agreement may be amended only by a written agreement signed by both parties.

9.3. **Waiver:** No waiver of any provision of this Agreement shall be effective unless in writing and signed by the party against whom the waiver is to be asserted. No waiver of any breach or default shall constitute a waiver of any subsequent breach or default.

9.4. **Severability:** If any provision of this Agreement is held to be invalid or unenforceable, the remaining provisions shall continue in full force and effect.

9.5. **Assignment:** Neither party may assign or transfer any rights or obligations under this Agreement without the prior written consent of the other party.

IN WITNESS WHEREOF, the parties have executed this Non-Disclosure Agreement as of the date first above written.

Attorney Intelligence LLP   **Moral Science Ltd.**

Signature: Signature:

Name: Name:

Title: Title:

Date: Date:

G. Important Provisions in Contracts:

1. Wavier Provision:

"**Waive**" means to give up a right.

A waiver is when one party voluntarily gives up a legal right, claim, or privilege. This provision adds extra protection to ensure the terms of the contract are enforceable. Most agreements include a no-waiver clause, which is standard.

A waiver involves surrendering a legal right, and the person giving up this right must be fully aware of it.
The purpose of a waiver or no-waiver clause in an agreement is to ensure that if a party fails to enforce its legal rights, whether intentionally or accidentally, it does not mean they are waiving those rights or remedies for a breach.

Example: A party might not strictly enforce an agreement's provisions in certain situations. For instance, they may accept late payments without charging penalties or late fees for a loyal customer. However, this does not mean they are waiving their rights under this agreement in the future.

2. Indemnification Provision in Contracts:

Indemnification is a legal promise where one party agrees to compensate other party for any losses, damages, or liabilities that occur because of certain actions by another party to the contract or by a third party or situations defined in a contract.

Here are examples:

a. **Broad Form Indemnification:** Offers the widest protection. It covers all losses, damages, and liabilities, regardless of their cause.

   Includes: Typically includes a "**duty to defend**" (the obligation to defend against claims) and a "**duty to hold harmless**" (protecting the other party from losses).

   Example: A company agrees to indemnify the customer for all losses related to the company's services, including any claims or legal costs, regardless of how the loss occurred.

b. Intermediate Indemnification: Provides protection but is more limited than broad form indemnification. It generally covers liabilities arising from the indemnitor's negligence, whether alone or with others.

Includes: Does not usually include the duty to defend; focuses more on holding the indemnitee harmless from negligence.

Example: A consultant agrees to protect the client from any liability caused by the consultant's own negligence while performing the agreed services.

c. Limited Indemnification: Offers the narrowest protection. It only covers specific liabilities directly resulting from the indemnitor's negligent performance of services.

Includes: Often does not include a duty to defend or broader protection; it is confined to negligence.

Example: A consultant agrees to indemnify the client only for liabilities directly caused by the consultant's negligence in their work.

In summary, Broad Form is the most comprehensive, Intermediate covers negligence to a lesser extent, and Limited is the most restrictive, focusing only on specific negligent acts.

Limiting the Scope of Indemnifications:

- Set time limits

- Specify maximum compensation amounts

- Define when these obligations start

- Limit the number of people protected

- Include mutual promises when needed.

Indemnification Clause:

Indemnification clauses are contractual provisions that outline financial protection and recovery if certain risks or events occur. These clauses are designed to handle specific risks or situations that might arise, which could otherwise be uncertain or unquantifiable.

Also known as **hold harmless agreements**, indemnification clauses shift the responsibility for certain liabilities from one party to another. They can be either mutual, where both parties agree to indemnify each other, or one-sided, where only one party provides indemnification.

Many businesses and organizations use these clauses to clearly define who is responsible for potential liabilities, helping to manage risk and clarify financial obligations related to the actions of each party involved.

Indemnification Clauses in Partnership Agreements: In partnership agreements, indemnification clauses are used to protect partners from personal liability arising from the actions of other partners. These clauses ensure that the personal actions or decisions of one partner—whether financial or legal—do not adversely affect the other partners. This helps maintain the stability of the partnership and allows the business to operate smoothly.

Indemnification Clauses in Insurance Agreements: Insurance policies often include indemnification clauses. When you buy insurance, the insurance company agrees to indemnify you (the policyholder) against specified damages or losses. This means the insurer will cover the costs or compensate for losses that you may incur, according to the terms of the policy.

Purpose of Indemnification Clauses:

The main goal of indemnification clauses is to protect one party from bearing the financial burden of another party's liabilities. They help clarify and limit how much one party is responsible for covering the losses or damages incurred by another party. While these clauses are commonly used in business relationships, they define specific boundaries and responsibilities to prevent excessive liability for either party.

Indemnification clauses are commonly used in real world under various contracts to protect the party being indemnified. Here are some practical examples:

Example 1: Service Provider Agreement:

A service provider includes an indemnification clause in their contract, requiring the customer to indemnify them against any losses or damages resulting from the misuse of the service provider's work product.

Example 2: Rental Car Agreement:

A car rental company includes an indemnification clause in their rental agreement, obligating the renter to indemnify the company for any damage to the vehicle that occurs during the rental period.

These clauses help manage and allocate risk by specifying who is responsible for covering potential losses or damages in specific situations.

Common Contracts with Indemnification Clauses:
Every contract is a good candidate for an indemnification clause. Common contracts with indemnification clauses include:

- Termination agreements
- Vendor agreements
- Noncompete agreements
- Sub-contractor agreements
- Employment contracts
- Construction contracts
- Partnership agreements

What happens if there is no indemnification clause?

Without an indemnification clause, both parties in a contract face increased risk if disputes arise. The party that suffers harm may have to bear more responsibility and could face unexpected third-party claims, leading to higher financial and legal exposure.

3. Limitation of liability:

Indemnification is a promise made by one party to compensate the other party for any losses, damages, or liabilities incurred.

Whereas, **Limitation of liability** (LOL) provisions restrict the amount one party must pay to the other if losses occur due to the contract. For these clauses to be enforceable, they must be reasonable and carefully drafted.

Tip: Always pay close attention to limitation of liability clauses whenever you enter into a contract to ensure they are fair and clearly defined.

Limitation of Liability Clause:

A limitation of liability clause is a provision in a contract that sets a cap on the amount one party has to pay the other if there are losses or damages resulting from the contract. This clause helps manage and mitigate the financial risks involved in commercial transactions.

Sources of Legal Liability:

All contracts, especially those involving commercial transactions, come with potential risks of liability. Legal liability can arise from several sources:

1. **Breach of Contract:**

   - Occurs when a party fails to fulfil their contractual obligations.

   - Example: A supplier fails to deliver goods on the agreed date.

2. **Negligence:**

   - Arises when a party's actions fail to meet a reasonable standard of care, causing harm.

   - **Example:** A car manufacturer like KIA designs a car with a defect, leading to an accident.

3. **Misrepresentation:**

   - Occurs when a party makes a false statement of fact that leads to the formation of a contract.

   - **Example:** A seller falsely claims their product meets certain quality standards.

4. **Infringement of Intellectual Property (IP) Rights:**

   - Happens when a party unlawfully uses another party's IP rights.

   - **Example:** A company uses another's patented technology without permission.

Understanding and incorporating limitation of liability clauses in contracts can help parties control their exposure to these risks and ensure that liabilities are manageable.

- A Limitation of Liability (LOL) clause serves to limit the amount and types of compensation one party can recover from the other party. It caps the liability incurred by one party and reduces the risk of a claim by the other party.

  Example: If a user of the Amazon Prime TV website suffers a loss because they relied on information provided on the site, a LOL clause in the website's terms and conditions could limit Amazon's liability, meaning the user can only recover up to a specified amount.

Need of Limitation of Liability Clause:

Limitation of liability (LOL) clauses are essential for managing the risks associated with a contract. Without such a clause, there is no cap on the financial damages one party can claim from the other. Including an express limitation of liability clause helps parties reduce their exposure to potential risks and financial liabilities that may arise under the contract.

Statutory (Law) Limits:

The law imposes certain restrictions on the application of limitation of liability clauses. Specifically, the extent to which liability can be limited often depends on whether the contract involves a consumer or not. Contracts involving consumers typically have stricter limitations and require the clauses to be fair and reasonable.

Business Contracts:

When a contract is between two businesses, limitation of liability clauses are regulated under the Unfair Contract Terms Act 1977 (UCTA). These clauses are prohibited in the following circumstances:

- **Death and Personal Injury Caused by Negligence:**

  Limitation clauses cannot exclude or limit liability for death or personal injury resulting from negligence.

- **Breach of Contract and Misrepresentation:**

  Liability for breach of contract and misrepresentation cannot be excluded entirely, but can be limited if the limitation is reasonable.

- **Breach of Implied Terms:**

  Terms implied by law, such as the quality and fitness for purpose of goods, must be upheld even if not expressly stated in the contract. However, liability for breaches of these terms can be limited if the limitation clause is reasonable.

- **Reasonableness Test:**

  For breaches of contract, misrepresentation, and breaches of implied terms, the limitation of liability clause must be 'reasonable' to be enforceable. Courts consider several factors to determine reasonableness, including:

Relative Bargaining Position:

Whether the parties had equal power to negotiate the terms of the contract.

Information Available at the Time of Contracting:

The knowledge each party had when the contract was made, including risks and potential liabilities.

Example:

A limitation clause that caps liability to the value of the contract is more likely to be deemed reasonable compared to a clause that excludes liability entirely. The courts look for fairness and balance in the limitation terms, ensuring neither party is unduly disadvantaged.

Consumer contracts:

Limitation of liability clauses in business-to-consumer contracts are generally less likely to be enforceable compared to those in business-to-business contracts. This is because any contractual provision that creates an imbalance between the parties to the detriment of the consumer is considered unfair and is prohibited.

- **Reasonableness Test:**

To be enforceable, a limitation of liability clause in a consumer contract must pass the reasonableness test, as described earlier. If a court determines that the restriction of liability is unreasonable, it will not be binding on the consumer. Factors considered in this test include:

- **Relative Bargaining Power:**

The consumer typically has less bargaining power compared to the business, making strict limitation clauses more likely to be seen as unfair.

- **Transparency and Clarity:**

The clause must be clearly communicated to the consumer and not hidden in fine print or complex language.

- **Implications:**

Businesses must ensure that limitation of liability clauses in consumer contracts are fair, transparent, and reasonable. Any attempt to unfairly limit liability at the consumer's expense will likely be struck down by the courts.

Drafting Your Limitation of Liability Clause:

To draft an effective limitation of liability (LOL) clause, it is crucial to accurately identify the risks associated with the contract and the potential losses that could arise. Consider the following questions during the drafting process:

- **What could possibly go wrong with this transaction?**

Identify all possible scenarios where things might not go as planned. Consider issues like delivery delays, quality problems, or service interruptions.

- **How likely is a breach of contract to happen?**
Assess the probability of each identified risk occurring. This will help prioritize which risks need more detailed attention in the clause.

- **How much might it cost? Could I afford it?**

  Estimate the potential financial impact of each risk. Consider whether your business can absorb these costs or if they would cause significant harm.

- **Are there any economic risks attached to this contract and/or to that particular industry?**

  Consider broader economic factors that might affect the contract, such as market volatility, regulatory changes, or industry-specific risks.

Steps to Draft a Limitation of Liability Clause:

- **Identify and List Potential Risks:**

  Clearly outline the risks you are concerned about, specific to the contract and industry.

- **Cap the Liability:**

  Specify a maximum amount that can be claimed for damages. This cap should be reasonable and proportionate to the value of the contract.

- **Define the Scope of Limitations:**

  Clearly state what types of losses are covered. For example, direct losses might be covered, but indirect or consequential losses might be excluded.

- **Include Exceptions:**

  Identify scenarios where the limitation of liability will not apply, such as cases of gross negligence, wilful misconduct, or fraud.

- **Ensure Compliance with Legal Standards:**

  Make sure the clause complies with relevant laws and regulations, particularly those that apply to consumer contracts if applicable.

By following these guidelines and considering the potential risks and costs, you can draft a limitation of liability clause that effectively manages risk while remaining fair and enforceable.

Limitation clause should set out:

(a) Unlimited Limitation of Liability (LOL):

Specify the losses each party agrees to compensate without limit. Examples include:

- Fraud

- Death and personal injury

- Breach of confidentiality

Example: Party A and Party B shall be liable without limit for losses arising from fraud, death or personal injury caused by negligence, and any breach of confidentiality obligations.

(b) Limited Limitation of Liability (LOL):

Define the losses each party agrees to cap and specify the amount of damages for which a party will be liable.

Clearly list which losses will be capped and the cap amount. The cap can vary for different types of losses and may be determined based on factors such as:

- The parties' level of insurance

- The value of the contract

- The potential amount of damage a breach of contract may cause

Example:

i.   Subject to subsection (a), the total liability of Party A for any claims, losses, damages, or expenses arising out of or in connection with this contract shall not exceed $1,00,000 USD or the total fees paid under this contract during the previous year.

ii.   The cap for liability related to breach shall be $5,00,000 USD.

iii. The cap for liability related to property damage shall be $2,00,000 USD.

(c) Excluded Losses:

Identify the specific losses that each party will not be liable for, such as:

- Loss of profit

- Loss of revenue

Note: Death and personal injury caused by negligence cannot be excluded from liability. Any clause attempting to exclude these will be unenforceable.

Example: Except as provided in subsection (a), neither party shall be liable for any indirect, incidental, consequential, or punitive damages, including but not limited to loss of profits, loss of revenue, or business interruption, even if advised of the possibility of such damages.
As a general rule, the liability cap should be capped to a reasonable amount, ensuring that a meaningful remedy is still available for the recovering party.

4. Warranty Vs Guarantee:

Warranty and Guarantee are terms often used interchangeably in everyday language, but they have distinct meanings, especially in legal and contractual contexts. Here's a breakdown of each:

Warranty

- **Definition:** A warranty is a formal promise or assurance made by a party (usually the seller or provider) regarding the quality, performance, or condition of a product or service. It generally involves specific terms and conditions that outline what is covered and for how long.

- **Purpose:** Warranties are intended to provide protection to the buyer or recipient by ensuring that the product or service meets certain standards. If the product or service fails to meet these standards, the warranty typically outlines how the issue will be addressed, such as through repair, replacement, or refund.

Types:

- **Express Warranty:** Clearly stated in a contract or agreement, detailing specific assurances about the product or service.

- **Implied Warranty:** Automatically applied by law, covering basic expectations such as merchantability (a product being fit for ordinary use) and fitness for a particular purpose.

- **Duration:** Warranties often have a specific time frame during which claims can be made. For example, a one-year warranty on a product.

Examples:

- A car manufacturer providing a 5-year warranty that covers repairs for defects in materials or workmanship.

- A software company offering a warranty that its product will function according to the specifications provided.

Guarantee

- **Definition:** A guarantee is a commitment or assurance, often more informal than a warranty, that a certain outcome or result will be achieved. It can also refer to a promise to rectify any issues if the product or service does not meet expectations.

- **Purpose:** Guarantees are typically used to provide additional confidence to the buyer or user that the product or service will perform as expected. They often involve a promise of satisfaction or a refund if the guarantee terms are not met.

Types:

- **Satisfaction Guarantee:** Ensures that the buyer will be satisfied with the product or service, with options for a refund or replacement if they are not.

- **Performance Guarantee:** Promises that the product or service will achieve certain performance levels or results.

- **Duration:** Guarantees can vary widely in terms of duration, from a short-term satisfaction guarantee to a longer-term performance guarantee.

Examples:

- A retailer offering a 30-day money-back guarantee if a customer is not satisfied with a product.

- A company guaranteeing that its cleaning service will meet specific cleanliness standards, or they will re-clean at no additional cost.

Key Differences

Formality:

1. **Warranty:** Usually a formal, legally binding promise with specific terms and conditions.

2. **Guarantee:** Often less formal and may be more focused on customer satisfaction or specific outcomes.

Scope:

1. **Warranty:** Covers defects or issues with the product or service, often with detailed repair or replacement procedures.

2. **Guarantee:** Focuses on ensuring satisfaction or achieving specific results, with less emphasis on detailed procedures.

Legal Implications:

1. **Warranty:** May be subject to specific legal requirements and protections, such as implied warranties under consumer protection laws.

2. **Guarantee:** Can be more flexible and may not always have the same legal backing as warranties.

In summary, while both warranties and guarantees serve to provide assurances about a product or service, warranties are typically more formal and detailed, focusing on specific coverage and remedies, whereas guarantees are often broader and more centred on ensuring overall satisfaction.

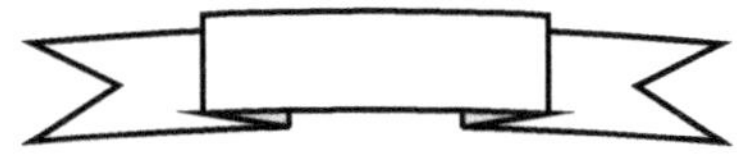